POSITIVE *Life* PRINCIPLES *for Women*

KAROL LADD

HARVEST HOUSE PUBLISHERS
EUGENE, OREGON

Cover by Koechel Peterson & Associates, Inc., Minneapolis, Minnesota

Cover photo © iStockphoto / Thinkstock

Back cover author photo © Shooting Starr Photography by Cindi Starr

Karol Ladd is published in association with the literary agency of the Steve Laube Agency, LLC, 5025 N. Central Ave. #635, Phoenix, AZ 85012.

POSITIVE LIFE PRINCIPLES FOR WOMEN
Copyright © 2013 by Karol Ladd
Published by Harvest House Publishers
Eugene, Oregon 97402
www.harvesthousepublishers.com

ISBN 978-0-7369-5011-4 (pbk.)
ISBN 978-0-7369-5012-1 (eBook)

Printed in China

13 14 15 16 17 18 19 20 21 / RDS-CD / 10 9 8 7 6 5 4 3 2

Contents

Introduction

Life Lessons from Slightly Imperfect People

Despise not the desert.
There is where God polishes his brightest gems.

R.A. TORREY

Our light and momentary troubles
are achieving for us an eternal glory
that far outweighs them all.

2 CORINTHIANS 4:17

If you are the type of person who hopes to learn from your mistakes and become stronger despite adversity, then this book is for you. We all stumble and make some not-so-great decisions now and then. Most of us face occasional and unexpected difficulties, but success in life is not based on how many potholes we fall into, but rather on how we learn and grow as we climb out of them.

The most positive people I know are the ones who take their blunders and challenges and turn them around to be stepping-stones for growth, change, and maturity. They choose to become better people as they work through glitches and jump over hurdles. To be quite honest, most of the strengths in my own life have developed as a result of the life lessons learned from the less-than-perfect scenarios in my life. In every mistake, every disappointment, and every trial, there are always new life principles to be gleaned and discovered in the process. These lessons can serve to make us wise, confident, and positive women.

What This Book Can Do for You

Each chapter in this book highlights a positive life principle you can apply to your life in a practical and personal way. The principles are gathered from the slightly imperfect lives of women in the Bible, as well as examples from people around us today. The transforming truths that can be learned from examples in the Bible reach to every age, faith, and social status. We can easily relate to the women whose stories were written centuries ago because, although society has changed, the needs of women have been constant. As women, we want to feel loved. We have fears, worries, and concerns. All women face discouragements at times. We often find ourselves dealing with difficult people. There are times of life when we grow tired and weary, and we tend to get down on ourselves quite easily.

This book is intended to bring hope, refreshment, and renewal to your slightly imperfect life. No one has her life all together, so let's get rid of that image in our minds. Let's not waste time wishing for what could have been—rather, let's take what we have and make it into the best it can be. Although adversities and disappointments may seem like a surprise to us, God is not surprised at all. He has a plan that goes beyond our frustrations, and He can transform our slightly imperfect situations into beautiful new landscapes. We can trust His goodness and faithfulness for the details of our lives. Life may not be good, but God is! He is a redeeming God, and He can bring beauty from ashes.

Taking Positive Steps

If your life is not the perfect picture you had planned, hold on to the hope and beauty of what you can learn as you press on in your journey. The enduring truths throughout these pages will give you inspiration and encouragement to make positive steps forward in your life. Each chapter ends with a Positive Life Strategy offering you a powerful truth, a plan of action to implement in your own life, and a "Pay It Forward" idea to reach out and bless someone else's life as a result of what you learned. I've also added an applicable verse to memorize so that you can carry the truths from this book with you continually throughout your life.

Even though this is a great individual read, you will also find that it makes a perfect group study. I've added a few discussion questions at the end of each chapter if you want to read it together with others. In the back you will find a quick two-page reference to the eight positive life principles you learn in this book, as well as a few additional books I recommend. My prayer is that as you apply the powerful principles in this book, you will also be a positive influence in the lives of those around you, elevating them to greater heights as well. Never underestimate the powerful ways God can use a positive woman to make a lasting difference in this world.

There are no lessons so useful as
those learned in the school of affliction.

J.C. RYLE

Chapter One

Listen to the Right Voices

*If you would voyage Godward, you must see
to it that the rudder of thought is right.*

W.J. Dawson

*Whatever is true, whatever is noble, whatever is right,
whatever is pure, whatever is lovely,
whatever is admirable—if anything
is excellent or praiseworthy—
think about such things.*

Philippians 4:8

What seems to be growing in the garden of your mind right now? Wouldn't it be wonderful if the thoughts in our minds resembled a lovely, well-kept garden full of refreshing, hope-filled thoughts—thoughts that always saw the best in others, our circumstances, and ourselves? The secret garden of our minds can flourish with vibrant, enriching colors, but so often the dull, monotonous weeds of discouragement, despair, and self-doubt seem to crowd out good and truthful thoughts. If we are not careful the weeds can take over our mind-gardens and we can grow into bitter, negative, joyless people. Thankfully, we can learn to be attentive to our thought life and the things our minds tend to dwell on. It is possible to weed out negative thinking and nurture life-giving truths instead.

Each day, seedling thoughts are continually planted in our minds—some good and some not-so-great. A critical family member, a hurtful co-worker, a past mistake, a frustrating disappointment can begin to dominate our minds and completely discourage us if we let it. It's easy to default to the negative. It happens quite naturally, just like weeds. That's why we must be diligent caretakers of our minds, planting good, healthy seeds and not allowing weeds of negativity and doubt to take over our brains. A.W. Tozer said, "What we think about when we are free to think about what we will—that is what we are or will soon become."[1] In other words, our thoughts soon become our actions. The mind is a powerful tool, and we can be transformed by the renewing of our minds.

⋘⋙

What voices are you listening to? What voices direct your life? Do those voices introduce truth, or do they insinuate fear, discouragement, and doubt? Perhaps you remember this old nursery rhyme:

> Mary, Mary, quite contrary,
> How does your garden grow?
> With silver bells, and cockle shells,
> And pretty maids all in a row.

There are numerous theories on what this quaint little rhyme was referring to, but we can use it as a reminder of the fact that we must carefully tend the garden of our mind to foster what is true, noble, right, pure, lovely, and admirable. Although Mary might have been quite contrary, antagonistic, and disagreeable, we don't have to be that way. Our mind-garden can be different depending on what we plant there. So we must ask ourselves, how does our garden grow? Are we planting seeds of truth or are we cultivating a garden based on assumptions and worries?

We can become extraordinary women simply by thinking above our daily circumstances. When we fill our minds with the truths that God is faithful and cares for the details of our lives, we begin to see life from a new perspective. We are able to have peace in the midst of the storm as we keep God's unfailing love at the forefront of our thoughts. Tozer also said, "What comes into our minds when we think about God is the most important thing about us." If we know and believe that God is truly good, then we recognize that even the challenges that come our way or the unanswered prayers in our lives are for a greater purpose than what we can see right now.

In the last few years the weather patterns in North America have been doing some crazy things. Huge killer tornadoes have bludgeoned the Southern and Midwestern states of the U.S. over and over again. One elderly couple in Alabama was highlighted in the news. The house in which they had been married and had spent all of their adult life and made all their family memories in had been completely demolished by one of the devastating storms. Finally, they had been able to rebuild again and were on their way to settling back into a semblance of the life they once knew, when another supercell storm system passed through and completely leveled their home again! When interviewed on the news, the wife gently expressed her frustration at the circumstance (and rightfully so), but then she added, "But I know that God has a bigger plan, and we're trusting Him through all of this."

Only a mind flourishing with a bountiful view of God's goodness and faithfulness can respond in such a positive way! Faith and hope were strong, sturdy flowers in the garden of this woman's mind and heart. I want to respond that way to life's challenges, don't you? Whether it is a small hurt from someone's misguided words or a huge, life-changing disaster, I want to respond with honest grief as well as a trusting grace and strength, rather than hopelessness and despair. It all begins in the mind as we consider who God is and how He interacts with us.

The Perfect Garden

Even if our life were wonderful and uncomplicated, it would still be possible to listen to the wrong voices. Take the perfect garden—the very first one—the Garden of Eden. Now if we lived in that garden, surely life would be perfect and we would have only lovely and faith-filled thoughts. Right? How could anything go wrong when you have the perfect circumstances, the perfect husband, the perfect relationship with God...not to mention the perfect body, the perfect garden, and the perfect meals every day? Eve was one woman who had it all! But oops—a seed of doubt was planted in her head, and she allowed it to grow and turn into sin.

Here's how the narrative unfolded.

> Now the serpent was more crafty than any of the wild animals the Lord God had made. He said to the woman, "Did God really say, 'You must not eat from any tree in the garden'?"
>
> The woman said to the serpent, "We may eat fruit from the trees in the garden, but God did say, 'You

must not eat fruit from the tree that is in the middle of the garden, and you must not touch it, or you will die.'"

"You will not certainly die," the serpent said to the woman. "For God knows that when you eat from it your eyes will be opened, and you will be like God, knowing good and evil."

When the woman saw that the fruit of the tree was good for food and pleasing to the eye, and also desirable for gaining wisdom, she took some and ate it. She also gave some to her husband, who was with her, and he ate it. Then the eyes of both of them were opened, and they realized they were naked; so they sewed fig leaves together and made coverings for themselves.[2]

Notice how Satan's subtle voice digs in and plants doubt: "You will not certainly die…For God knows that when you eat from it your eyes will be opened, and you will be like God, knowing good and evil." The little doubt seed was planted. The seed that says, "Does God really love you? If He loved you He wouldn't keep you from eating the fruit from that tree. No—He is only looking out for Himself and doesn't want you to be like Him. He is not looking out for your best interest, but only His. You can't trust His love and His care for you if He is going to deny you the privilege of eating that fruit." So Eve listened to the voice of doubt instead of trusting God's loving care. She allowed the little seedling to grow into action, and all humanity fell as a result.

The seed of truth has a different voice. Truth says, "God loves you and knows what is best for you. He has given you everything you need to satisfy your heart's desire. Trust His love for you, and trust that He knows what is best." Oh, the beautiful flowers that grow in the mind of the one who listens to the voice of truth! Her life is filled with peace in knowing that God loves her and is watching out for her. He is her keeper. Her life is filled with joy, recognizing that He has redeemed her and set her free from the power of sin through Christ. Her life is filled with hope as she looks forward to the glories of heaven beyond this world. The seeds of truth found in the rich soil of God's Word create the loveliest gardens this world has ever seen.

How Does Your Garden Grow?

Which voices creep into your mind? Maybe one of them is the voice of fear that whispers, *What if this happens?* Or perhaps it's the voice of self-doubt, which scolds you and says, *You've made so many stupid mistakes before—you can't do anything right.* Maybe it's the voice of contempt, which continually beats you up as it snarls, *You're too fat. You're too ugly. No one likes you. God probably made a mistake when He made you.* The voices we hear take on many forms and fashions, but we don't have to allow them to plant weeds that will take over our minds. Instead, we can pull those weeds out by the roots and replace these thoughts with the seeds of truth.

I like to use a little three-step process when it comes to changing my thinking: *recognize, root out,* and *replace.* Three R's to right thinking. It's amazing how quickly a weed can grow in our minds without us even realizing it. When it comes to the real flower garden that's in front of our house, I think weeds pop up literally overnight. Given a few days, some of those pesky plants can grow to become the size of small trees! So we must be vigilant and alert, recognizing the weeds when they first appear. The apostle Peter (who knew a few things about temptation, as he himself was first tempted and then denied he knew Christ) wrote, "Stay alert! Watch out for your great enemy, the devil. He prowls around like a roaring lion, looking for someone to devour."[3]

It's inevitable—doubts, discouragement, and lies will pop into our heads. How do we recognize them? We need to take a moment to consider our own personal reoccurring thoughts—the ones that seem to grow in our own garden. Myself, I struggled many years with self-doubt in every area of my life, from my physical appearance to my capabilities to my relationships.

I first needed to recognize that these were unhealthy and destructive thoughts. They were doing me more harm than good. Often we grow comfortable with our fears and doubts, and we fail to identify them as weeds. We must recognize they are not based on God's truth, and they drain the joyfulness from our lives. These negative thoughts also prevent good seeds from growing.

Stop for a moment and consider, what are some of the destructive voices you are allowing to grow in your mind? What are some of the same fears you keep rehearsing? A good indicator of some of your weedy thinking is to consider what the topic of your last argument with someone was. Often arguments have our weedy thinking at the core. Recognize the faulty thinking for what it is, and also recognize that it is distracting you and others from your beautiful attributes that are ready to grow and flourish. Worse, faulty thinking can destroy those attributes.

Rooting Out the Weeds

Once you begin to recognize your own personal brain-weeds,

then it is time to root them out. If you have ever tended a garden you know that if you just whack weeds off at the surface, they will return. You must dig them out by the roots! Eve should have rooted out the voice of the enemy by getting to the core problem. It wasn't really about the fruit—rather, it was about doubting God's goodness and care for her.

The core issue was Eve's lack of trust in God's love for her. He had given her every tree in the perfect garden except the tree of the knowledge of good and evil. He did this for her and Adam's own good, to protect them. But instead of focusing on God's goodness, care, and provision, Eve started thinking He was holding something back from her. She believed the lie that He didn't love her and was denying her the best. Yet God's love and truth says to us, "I have given you everything you need." The voice of doubt says, "God doesn't love you. Look what He's keeping from you."

What is at the root of the negative voices that pop into your head? Dig deep for a minute and consider it. With my own self-doubts, as I asked God to reveal to me what was deep in my heart, I began to realize there were quite a few core issues. One was my fear of the unknown and lack of trust that He would really take care of me no matter what happened in my life. I also realized I had made my own reputation into an idol in my mind. I wanted everyone to like me, and I couldn't stand the thought of someone finding out I had flaws. I saw that trusting God means trusting Him to care for me no matter what happens. Trusting Him also means believing that He made me and formed me—and that He didn't make a mistake. It means trusting Him to protect my reputation and honor.

We are His workmanship, created for good works. He has a plan for us, and He is our Good Shepherd who leads us and guides us along the way in that plan as we look to Him. The Bible reminds us that it is God who is at work in us both to will and to act in order to fulfill His good purpose.[4] We are masterpieces created in Christ Jesus for good works which God has prepared beforehand so that we should walk in them. Yes, He truly does have a good purpose for us, because He loves us. Ultimately, when I dug to the root of the voices I tend to listen to, the roots looked very similar to Eve's roots—I doubted God's goodness and unfailing love toward me.

Dealing with the root system of the weeds in my mind allowed me to dig them up, confess them to our loving heavenly Father, and then turn in a new direction. I needed to replace the old ugly weeds with healthy, vibrant truth. What is the truth that I do know about God? The Bible reveals that He is love. His very nature is love. He is good, and He is faithful. He is able to do all things. Oh, what powerful and life-changing seeds we plant in our brain when we know God's Word!

Consider the following seeds from the twenty-third psalm, which can grow into beautiful flowering plants, not only transforming our actions and words, but also how we react to our circumstances.

> The LORD is my shepherd;
>> I have all that I need.
> He lets me rest in green meadows;
>> he leads me beside peaceful streams.
>> He renews my strength.
> He guides me along right paths,
>> bringing honor to his name.
> Even when I walk

through the darkest valley,
I will not be afraid,
    for you are close beside me.
Your rod and your staff
    protect and comfort me.
You prepare a feast for me
    in the presence of my enemies.
You honor me by anointing my head with oil.
    My cup overflows with blessings.
Surely your goodness and unfailing love will pursue me
    all the days of my life,
and I will live in the house of the LORD forever.[5]

What rich treasures are found in this psalm, one of God's love letters to us! What a beautiful reminder of the faithful care our heavenly Father has for us. Soak in the words: "Surely your goodness and unfailing love will pursue me all the days of my life." Allow the seeds of His unfailing love to be planted in your heart and mind. Jesus said, "As the Father has loved me, so have I loved you. Now remain in my love."[6] There is great peace and joy when we remain conscious and aware of His love. Reflect upon it. Dwell on it. Live life with the constant reassurance and confidence that God generously offers His unfailing love toward His children—those who believe in Christ.

❧

Jesus reminded us that He is the vine and we are the branches. If we abide in Him, and He in us, we will bear much fruit. Abiding in Him means dwelling or remaining in Him. He added that without Him we can do nothing.

I encourage you to draw close to God and allow His words to fill your mind and heart. As we get to know His Word, we can recognize His voice more clearly. We can also pray that He will make us alert to recognize the enemy's voice of discouragement and despair. Fill the garden of your mind with the trustworthy seeds of God's Word and you are sure to have a harvest of lasting and lovely fruit.

We are not alone in tending our garden. Jesus not only identified Himself as the true vine, but He also said that God, our Father, is the Gardener. As we abide in Christ, there are times when the Father may gently and kindly do some pruning to help us grow even more fruitful. Pruning is necessary for a grapevine to grow stronger and healthier as a plant. Let us trust the hands of our good Gardener—He knows what is best for us. Even when we walk through difficulties, His love does not fail. Continue to dwell on His sovereignty and faithfulness both in the good times and bad. Don't allow the doubting voice to begin to grow in your mind. Instead, listen to the voice of truth, which says, "See how very much our Father loves us, for he calls us his children, and that is what we are!"[7]

===== *Positive Life Strategy* =====

Positive Truth

We have a choice about the voices we will listen to in our minds. Cultivate the voice of truth and allow it to grow.

Plan of Action

1. Recognize discouraging and doubt-filled voices.

2. Root out the negative voices by getting to the core issue.

3. Replace the negative voices with God's truth.

Pay It Forward

Give someone a mental bouquet of flowers today through your sincere words of strength and courage. Think of someone you know who needs to be reminded of God's love. Write them a note or e-mail them and include several verses of Scripture, giving them good seeds of truth to plant in their mind-garden. I recommend Psalm 23, Psalm 103, and Romans 8:31-39.

Place It in Your Heart

Do not conform to the pattern of this world,
but be transformed by the renewing of your mind.
Then you will be able to test and approve what God's will is—
his good, pleasing and perfect will.

Romans 12:2

Discussion Starters

- What are some of the typical negative weeds women tend to allow to grow in their minds?

- What are some practical ways we can replace them with seeds of beauty and truth?

Chapter Two

Look for the Possibilities

Great opportunities come to all,
but many do not know they have met them.
The only preparation to take advantage of them
is simple fidelity to watch what each day brings.

ALBERT E. DUNNING

Nothing is impossible with God.

LUKE 1:37 NLT

It seems ironic that a blind woman would point people in a positive direction, helping them find clarity and vision for their lives. Helen Keller didn't let her challenges keep her from looking at the possibilities in her own life. Born in 1880, she became both blind and deaf at 19 months of age due to a childhood illness. Yet she was the first blind and deaf woman to earn a bachelor of arts degree, and she authored a dozen books and numerous other writings. In her book *We Bereaved* she wrote, "When one door of happiness closes, another opens; but often we look so long at the closed door that we do not see the one which has been opened for us."

Where are you looking? Have you allowed your eyes to zoom in on the frustrations that are right in front of you, making them seem larger than life? Or are you looking at the bigger, broader picture—the picture that includes possibilities and hope? There are always possibilities around the corner, but we need to be looking for them instead of dwelling on what we don't have. I like to say that the "B" in Plan B stands for beautiful. Often we think our Plan A was the perfect plan and that Plan B is second-rate. Have you ever considered that our Plan B is actually God's Plan A, and He can do a great work despite our disappointments and even our mistakes?

It may be difficult to conceive in your mind that anything good could come from hurt, pain, and loss, whether it is a physical, financial, or family problem in your life. We must be honest and grieve through the sadness that life brings. We don't want to ignore the disappointment and hurt in our heart, but we also don't want to close our mind's eye to the redemption God can bring in the toughest of situations. It may take time and perseverance. Plan B may be difficult, but that doesn't mean it isn't doable. Perhaps the "B" in Plan B means "Be patient." Allow God to do His work in His way, and do not despair—for there is always hope.

In the Pit

When we are in the pit, it is difficult to see anything but the pit. Did you ever notice that there are several instances in the Bible where people were in literal pits? Think about it. Joseph was thrown in a pit by his brothers and then eventually sold into slavery. Not the Plan A Joseph had for his life. And then there's the little-known story of Benaiah, who ended up in a pit with a lion. Seriously! The Bible tells us that he was a valiant warrior and performed many great exploits. The prophet Samuel recorded that Benaiah "struck down Moab's two mightiest warriors. He also went down into a pit on a snowy day and killed a lion."[1] Now that probably wasn't on his schedule of things to do that day either.

David described God as the one who "redeems your life from the pit."[2] Now perhaps you have felt as though your life or your day was in the pits and you could see no hope, no redemption, and no way out. I suppose that's how pit-dweller Jeremiah felt. Jeremiah was one of God's prophets who was thrown into a pit as a result of simply proclaiming what God told him to say. That doesn't seem right! There he was, obeying God, and he was thrown into a pit. Take a look at how low this Old Testament prophet must have felt: "The thought of my suffering and homelessness is bitter beyond words. I will never forget this awful time, as I grieve over my loss."[3]

But Jeremiah didn't call it quits. He was able to keep his eyes on the Lord despite his circumstances. Here's what he said after describing his situation:

> Yet I still dare to hope when I remember this: The faithful love of the LORD never ends! His mercies never cease. Great is his faithfulness; his mercies begin afresh each morning. I say to myself, "The LORD is my inheritance; therefore, I will hope in him!" The LORD is good to those who depend on him, to those who search for him.[4]

Now there's a person who has his eyes in a positive direction! He's not dwelling on his dismal circumstances in the pit—instead he is dwelling on the Lord's faithfulness. His sight is going beyond what he can see, and is looking to the hope of what a faithful God can do. How's your eyesight? In one of his most fearful moments David declared, "Those who look to him are radiant; their faces are never covered with shame."[5] Oh, for the faith to look past the dark clouds of despair and see the sunlight of God's faithfulness peeking through to bring us comfort and hope!

Laughter Instead of Looking

As we consider another slightly imperfect example from the Bible, Sarah, we can readily see why her hope was a little diminished. The Lord had promised her a son, but she was 90 years old and her husband was 100. Hmm…I can't really fault her for faltering a little in her faith. To be quite honest, I've had less faith when I'm simply praying for God to renew my strength after a work-weary day.

To set the stage, God had earlier promised Abraham (Sarah's husband) that he would be a great nation, but the only problem was that even then Abraham and Sarah were quite old and without children. So Sarah figured she needed to help God out and find her own solution. She gave her handmaiden, Hagar, over to Abraham so that she would have a descendant for them. Really not a good idea. Let's just say it didn't work out so well in the family dynamics, and was a cause for conflict rather than resolution.

But God had a different plan—a good plan—Plan A. The Bible tells us that He came and visited Abraham again and told him that Sarah would have a child. Here's the account of the story found in Genesis:

> "Where is Sarah, your wife?" the visitors asked.
>
> "She's inside the tent," Abraham replied.
>
> Then one of them said, "I will return to you about this time next year, and your wife, Sarah, will have a son!"

Sarah was listening to this conversation from the tent. Abraham and Sarah were both very old by this time, and Sarah was long past the age of having children. So she laughed silently to herself and said, "How could a worn-out woman like me enjoy such pleasure, especially when my master—my husband—is also so old?"

Then the LORD said to Abraham, "Why did Sarah laugh? Why did she say, 'Can an old woman like me have a baby?' Is anything too hard for the LORD? I will return about this time next year, and Sarah will have a son."

Sarah was afraid, so she denied it, saying, "I didn't laugh."

But the LORD said, "No, you did laugh."[6]

Don't you just love it? Just picture arguing with the Lord! "I didn't laugh." "Yes, you did." This story makes me chuckle every time I read it, but only because I can see myself doing the same thing. Isn't God's gracious love so very beautiful? Did you pay attention to the words "Is anything too hard for the LORD?" Despite her doubts, God gave Sarah a wonderful son named Isaac, through whose line He would eventually send His Son, Jesus.

Like Sarah, so often my eyes are on my circumstances, and I take my eyes off of God's power. I so easily forget that He is able to do whatever He wants. If He can refresh a barren womb, He can restore the broken pieces in my life as well. It may not be in the form or fashion I think it will happen, but I—we—must never lose sight of the fact that nothing is too hard for Him. May we always keep in clear focus the God who can do immeasurably more than we ask or imagine.

As believers in Christ, we may not be able to see the perfect outcome or the beauty in Plan B, but we can always trust God's faithfulness and power. Even if all does not turn out as we hoped or dreamed, even if we never seem to see a nice pretty bow that ties up all the difficulties in our life into a lovely package—we do know that this is not all there is. Ultimately the greatest hope in life is not in this world—rather it is the life we look forward to in eternity with Christ. Bright hope for tomorrow points ultimately to that hope, our eternal hope where the possibilities are endless.

Take heart, my friend. Your situation or your marriage or your job or your child may seem hopeless. Turn your eyes upward! Take your focus off of the pit you are in and put your hope in a faithful God, who loves you and cares about the details of your life. There is nothing too difficult for Him.

Certainly we must be realistic and grieve the hurt or disappointment or loss of the old dream of what we thought life should look like. However, as we work through the loss of the old dream, let us turn our eyes to the possibilities in front of us. May God renew our strength, refresh our hope, and direct our steps as we keep our eyes on Him. He is faithful, and He is able.

Possibilities in the Midst of Discouragement

It can be a little discouraging when you try to sell your home three different times and no one even puts down an offer. Jennifer and Steve were about to give up hope of ever moving out of their neighborhood, which had become increasingly dangerous with most of the houses falling into a state of disrepair. On top of that, without warning Steve was laid off from his job, which he thought he would have forever. With a family of four to feed, he jumped right into the job hunt and by God's grace was able to find a position in a nearby town immediately.

There was only one problem; the family would need to move. Since they had tried to sell their home several times before without success, the possibilities seemed rather grim. But with God all things are possible. They began praying that if God wanted Steve to take this job, He would bring a buyer for their home. They put it in His hands, knowing it would be a miracle if they could sell their home after so many failed attempts. Well, it must have been in His plan for them to move, because within one week of putting the house on the market, they had three offers. Three! Sometimes God allows us to get to the place of bleakness so that we can see His power at work.

I'm reminded of an incident in the life of Jesus. When Lazarus, the brother of Mary and Martha, was very ill, Jesus did not go immediately to help. No, He waited and allowed Lazarus to die, so that the power of God might be revealed. Let us not think that because we are waiting God is not at work. He has a plan. And sometimes our seemingly unanswered prayers are a time of waiting, so that we may more clearly see His great hand at work. Trust Him even when you don't see the possibilities. Trust Him even as you wait and pray. His plan is bigger and better. He is able to do far more than we can ask or imagine.

Where is your focus? Is it on your frustrations, or is it on the faithfulness of the Lord? Let us raise our eyes and set our sight on the One who is able to bring life and hope to places that seem dark and dead.

Let's set our eyes on the possibilities, seeking God's direction and not our own silly plans. How wonderful to watch His Plan A unfold before our eyes as we keep our focus on Him!

===================== *Positive Life Strategy* =====================

POWERFUL TRUTH

In every challenge we face, there are also possibilities waiting to be discovered.

PLAN OF ACTION

1. Grieve the loss of the plan you thought was perfect.

2. Ask God to open your eyes to what He can do.

3. Wait patiently.

4. Trust His faithfulness.

5. Keep your eyes on the Shepherd and ask Him to lead you.

6. Take steps forward as He guides.

PAY IT FORWARD

Do you know someone who is in a pit and doesn't seem to see any possibilities? Jump into their pit with them and let them know you are there for them. Allow them to cry or grieve if they need to and offer to pray with them. Brainstorm together and help them to turn their focus onto the possibilities. Encourage them with the truth that nothing is too hard for God. Help them think through the next steps, and share with them the hope that comes in trusting His love and faithfulness.

Place It in Your Heart

Is anything too hard for the Lord?

Genesis 18:14

Discussion Starters

- Why does our focus make such a difference in our attitude toward our circumstances?

- Describe a time in your life when the odds were against you. How did you find hope?

Chapter Three

Guard Against Comparisons

The prosperity of those to whom we wish well
can never grieve us;
And the mind which is bent on doing good to all
can never wish ill to any.

MATTHEW HENRY

Let us run with perseverance the race marked out for us,
fixing our eyes on Jesus,
the pioneer and perfecter of faith.

HEBREWS 12:1-2

If you have ever watched any of the Olympic track-and-field events, you know that a split second makes all the difference, especially in sprint races. If a competitor in the 100-meter sprint takes even part of a second to glance at the runners on either side of her—she's lost the race.

In life as well as in running, we must learn to keep our eyes on our own race and not become distracted by comparing ourselves with others. Easier said than done, right? As women, we so quickly begin to compare with the other women around us. Often it happens the moment we walk into a room with others. *Am I as thin as she is? Do I fit in here? Why can't my hair look as good as hers does? I wish I had her complexion.*

It's a trap each one of us can easily stumble into, and in the process we become dissatisfied with who we are and what God has planned for us. We tend to lose sight of what our purpose is in life. Perhaps that's why the apostle Paul, with his powerfully purpose-filled life, was able to say, "I press on toward the goal to win the prize for which God has called me heavenward in Christ Jesus."[1] Just as a sprinter keeps her eye on the goal or the finish line, so we need to keep our eyes fixed on the purpose God has given us and not be distracted by envy, jealousy, or comparison. True maturity is when we can look with joy at how God is blessing others and be sincerely thankful for the way He uses each one of us in a variety of ways and in different styles.

There is only one you. God made you with a unique set of gifts and talents and with a distinct purpose in this world. When we keep our eyes on the fact that He is at work in and through us to accomplish what He put us on this earth to do, we begin to feel a joyful confidence. We can rejoice in our assignment in the big scheme of life. On the other hand, when we start looking at everyone else and begin to compare ourselves with others, we become either prideful or jealous. Comparisons tend to rob us of our strength, distract us from our purpose, and throw us off course from our goals.

Family Comparisons

Perhaps you are familiar with the story of two sisters, Rachel and Leah, in the Bible. Rachel was beautiful in form and appearance, the Bible tells us, but Leah, well...the Bible simply tells us she had weak eyes. The Hebrew word for weak, *rak*, means "tender, soft, faint-hearted, or gentle." It doesn't necessarily mean that Leah was ugly, but we do know that Rachel was attractive to Jacob and had captured his heart.

The Scripture says that Jacob loved Rachel and wanted to marry her. Laban, Rachel's father, had promised to give her to Jacob in marriage, but he tricked Jacob into marrying Leah first. One week later, Jacob married Rachel too. Now Jacob had two wives, one who was cherished and one who was not. Leah was the first to have children. God allowed her to have boy after boy after boy after boy, which was a good thing because it allowed her to gain prominence in the family despite being the "unloved wife."

Here's an account of the names Leah gave her sons. Read each explanation she gives as she reveals her hurting heart as a result of comparing herself with her sister:

> Leah became pregnant and gave birth to a son. She named him Reuben, for she said, "It is because the LORD has seen my misery. Surely my husband will love me now."
>
> She conceived again, and when she gave birth to a son she said, "Because the LORD heard that I am not loved, he gave me this one too." So she named him Simeon.
>
> Again she conceived, and when she gave birth to a son she said, "Now at last my husband will become attached to me, because I have borne him three sons." So he was named Levi.
>
> She conceived again, and when she gave birth to a son she said, "This time I will praise the LORD." So she named him Judah.[2]

Rachel, despite having the attention and love of her husband, began in turn to compare herself to Leah. She became jealous, angry, and demanding. Here's how she so lovingly and respectfully approached her husband about the matter:

> When Rachel saw that she was not bearing Jacob any children, she became jealous of her sister. So she said to Jacob, "Give me children, or I'll die!"
>
> Jacob became angry with her and said, "Am I in the place of God, who has kept you from having children?"[3]

Well, it appears she was a little short on love and respect when she demanded a child from Jacob. Instead of turning her eyes to the Lord, she turned her demands toward her husband. I can't point the finger at her. I'm just as guilty of trying to make people meet my needs instead of looking first to God for my help. It's interesting, but when I turn my eyes on the Lord first, things seem to fall into a beautiful perspective. When I'm consumed with envy or comparisons, I become very shortsighted. How about you?

The tally of kids between the two sisters was slightly lopsided. Leah had seven (six boys and a girl) and Rachel had zero. On the other hand, Rachel was loved and Leah was not. Each sister wanted what the other sister had. Both sisters had blessings in their lives, but their focus was on what they didn't have. The Bible tells us that eventually God listened to Rachel and opened her womb. She had a son and said, "God has taken away my reproach." She named her son Joseph, saying, "May the LORD add to me another son!" Do you get a sense by that wish that she is still gripped by the competition with her sister? Poor Joseph. She didn't imply that she was thrilled or satisfied with him. She was more concerned with having more kids and catching up with her sister. Instead of rejoicing about what she had been given, her mind was on more, *more, MORE*.

Oh, the ugliness of envy!

Your Divine Purpose

Can you blame Leah and Rachel for the family feud? I know that on the surface it seems almost justified that they should have rivalry between them. But God did not create us to live in the dark dungeon of comparisons, anger, jealousy, envy, and discontentment. No, every one of us was created for a divine purpose. He has given us a unique assignment that only we can carry out. Augustine wrote, "Thou hast formed us for Thyself, and our hearts are restless till they find rest in Thee." Often we become restless with comparisons and rivalry when we lose sight of the fact that God has a beautiful plan that He wants to carry out in *our* lives and no one else's life. His unique plan includes both triumphs and challenges.

Take Leah, for instance. Sadly, she was not loved by Jacob as much as Rachel was loved by him, but God gifted her in a different way. He allowed her to have many sons, which elevated her status within the family. He took care of her and honored her, despite the pain and heartache she experienced. After Leah's sixth son was born she said, "God has endowed me with a good endowment." Now if she had simply stopped her little speech right there, it would have seemed she was content with what God had given her. Yet she went on to say, "Now my husband will honor me, because I have borne him six sons." She still wanted what she didn't have! She continued to crave her husband's attention.

To be quite honest, doesn't every wife deeply desire her husband's attention? We can sympathize with her pain. Sadly, many women throughout the ages and even today live in homes where they do not feel loved or valued. Perhaps that's how you feel right now in your own life. I wonder what life would have been like for Leah if she had taken her eyes off her husband and turned them on the Lord instead. My friend, may we look to the Lord to satisfy the longings of our hearts. His love can satisfy us in a way that human love cannot. No human love is perfect, but God's love is unfailing and complete.

Charles Spurgeon said, "The cure for envy lies in living under a constant sense of the divine presence, worshipping God and communing with him all the day long, however long the day may seem."[4] Let us worship Him in the midst of our heartaches and longings and watch Him work in mysterious and glorious ways.

Sometimes we must wait on His timing. Rachel had to watch her sister give birth to seven children before she had one of her own. Waiting is hard, but God can teach us and prepare us here. However, when we are in the waiting room is one of those times when comparisons can grab us, knock us down, and discourage us. It's hard when we see everyone else getting married or having babies or getting the promotion at work. Waiting on the Lord requires a constant trust that God has not stopped working—that He has a good plan and His timing is better than our own.

We may have some tough times. Our life may not seem as perfect as someone else's, but are we able to rejoice in what God has given us? Rachel and Leah had both been given good gifts, but instead of rejoicing in the Lord, they lived under the burden of comparisons. When Paul encouraged believers to "rejoice in the Lord always," he didn't tell us to rejoice in circumstances. He told us to turn our focus onto the Lord, for we can always rejoice in Him. Think about a woman who is rejoicing in the power and wisdom of the Lord, thanking Him for all He is able to do and praising Him for His loving-kindness in her life. Competing with others doesn't factor into this woman's life. She has her eyes on God's good plan, and not on what He is doing in other people's lives.

The only time we should be looking at others is when we are looking in compassion, not in comparison. Compassion says, "I love you and want to help you. I feel with you." Comparison says, "I'm thinking of myself and want to be better than you." Let us be filled with compassion, not filled with comparisons.

In Romans we read, "Rejoice with those who rejoice, weep with those who weep."[5] When something good happens to another person, we ought to rejoice with them and be glad for all God is doing as He carries out His unique plan in their lives. Think about what it must have been like in Jacob's camp when Leah had her first son. I wonder if Rachel gave her a baby shower or brought a bunch of baby gifts for her sister. Probably not. I doubt if she even brought over dinner or offered to babysit. No, I'm guessing Rachel stewed in jealousy, which grew and grew as Leah's family portrait grew.

As much as we want life to be fair and everyone to have everything even-steven, that's not the way life works out, and that's not the way God deals with us. I'm in a delightful group called Christian Women in Media (CWIMA) and although the group is filled with powerhouse women in all forms of media, there is a beautiful spirit within it. There is a sense of building each other up rather than competing against one another. We sincerely elevate and encourage one another, and I believe it is a result of our common love for the Lord within the group. It would be easy to compare with other women's success and begin to feel like a failure, but when our eyes are on God's plan we can rejoice about how He uses each one of us.

❧

You have unique gifts, talents, and abilities to offer this world. God has equipped you with a plan designed just for you to carry out in your life. Let us delight in what God has purposed for each one of our lives, because ultimately our life fits into His divine plan for this world. We can take joy in what He is doing in other women's lives because we know there is a bigger picture. Whenever you feel that temptation to compare with others and begin to feel discouraged or afraid, turn your eyes to the God who sees all and knows all. He has a beautiful design just for you. Wait patiently for Him. Your story is not finished.

Positive Life Strategy

Positive Truth

God has a unique plan for each one of us, which He carries out using the gifts and talents He has given us.

Plan of Action

1. Guard your mind against comparing with others by turning your focus upward.

2. Ask for God's help and direction as you use your unique gifts and talents.

3. Open your eyes to the blessings that God has given you right now.

4. Thank Him for His unique plan for your life every day.

5. Rejoice in who the Lord is and the work He is doing in you as well as in others.

6. Be happy with others for the good things happening in their lives.

Pay It Forward

Celebrate someone else's success by letting them know that you are rejoicing with them. Write them a note, bring them flowers, or do something kind for them as you give thanks for the wonderful and unique plan God has for their life. Consider someone who has recently experienced a blessing in their life—perhaps an achievement, an honor, or a promotion. Maybe it is someone who has just gotten married or had a new baby. You may even want to consider someone who has sparked a slight bit of jealousy in your mind. Determine to be truly happy for them and honor them for the good that has come to them.

Place It in Your Heart

Let all that I am wait quietly before God,
for my hope is in him.

Psalm 62:5 NLT

Discussion Starters

- Why do you think it is so tempting for women to compare themselves with others?

- What are some ways we can actively keep our eyes on the plan God has for us?

Chapter Four

Be an Encourager,
Not a Discourager

I wonder why it is that we are not all kinder to each other...
How much the world needs it!
How easily it is done!

HENRY DRUMMOND

Do not let any unwholesome talk come out of your mouths,
but only what is helpful for building
others up according to their needs,
that it may benefit those who listen.

EPHESIANS 4:29

Paula was enthusiastic about her new opportunity to volunteer at the Downtown Women's Shelter, and she couldn't wait to share her passion with her friends at lunch. Her friend Debbie spoke up immediately. "What in the world are you thinking? Why would you devote ten hours a week to *that* cause when you could do something closer to home?" Bridget chimed in. "Yeah, why don't you just donate some old clothes or give away some canned goods rather than tire yourself out with extra stuff to do? You're doing too much already!" Then Nancy added in a sharp tone, "Don't you know how dangerous it is in that part of town? Why would you risk going there when there are so many fun things to do on this side of the city?"

Needless to say, Paula's optimism was soon deflated and so was her passion for helping the homeless. Although she had carefully planned and prayed about how she could devote her time and talent to something more meaningful than simply going to social meetings at the country club, she was now second-guessing herself as a result of her friends' frivolous evaluations. She began questioning her own sense of judgment...but perhaps she should have been questioning her choice of friends.

It's amazing how much power and influence other people's words can have on our hearts. Certainly constructive criticism has its place and can be a vital tool when making a decision or considering a new idea. On the other hand, a constant spirit of criticism can dry up dreams, crush creativity, and hinder growth and progress. Our words are powerful and can be used for good or for destruction. Encouraging words can go a long way in helping someone move in a positive direction and giving them strength for the rough roads ahead. Which kind of woman are you? Are you an encourager, or are you a discourager?

Be Careful What You Say

We find a little story tucked away in the book of Numbers in the Old Testament that gives us a healthy warning about what we allow to come out of our mouths. Moses was God's chosen leader to guide the Israelites out of captivity and into the Promised Land, but there were some discouragers along the way. Sadly, two of the discouragers were Moses' own brother and sister. They decided to focus on one perceived shortcoming in their brother's life—his foreign wife. Ultimately they were really questioning his authority, which possibly stemmed from hearts steeped in jealousy or envy of their brother's leadership position. Here's how the narrative unfolds:

> While they were at Hazeroth, Miriam and Aaron criticized Moses because he had married a Cushite woman. They said, "Has the LORD spoken only through Moses? Hasn't he spoken through us, too?" But the LORD heard them. (Now Moses was very humble—more humble than any other person on earth.)[1]

I think it is important to note the words, "The LORD heard them." Often we don't think about the fact that God hears what we say and He is well aware of the ugliness that comes out of our mouths. Solomon said the fear of the Lord is the beginning of wisdom. It is fearful and convicting to think that the God of love and Creator of all things hears my unkind criticism or rude comments. One way to keep our speech pure is to ask the Lord to guard our mouths and remember that He is the God who sees all and hears what comes out of our mouths. Now let's get back to the story:

> So immediately the LORD called to Moses, Aaron, and Miriam and said, "Go out to the Tabernacle, all three of you!" So the three of them went to the Tabernacle. Then the LORD descended in the pillar of cloud and stood at the entrance of the Tabernacle. "Aaron and Miriam!" he called, and they stepped forward. And the LORD said to them, "Now listen to what I say:
>
> If there were prophets among you,

> I, the Lord, would reveal myself in visions.
> I would speak to them in dreams.
> But not with my servant Moses.
>   Of all my house, he is the one I trust.
> I speak to him face to face,
>   clearly, and not in riddles!
>   He sees the Lord as he is.
> So why were you not afraid
>   to criticize my servant Moses?
>
> The Lord was very angry with them, and he departed.
> As the cloud moved from above the Tabernacle, there
> stood Miriam, her skin as white as snow from leprosy. [2]

God chose to work immediately and dramatically to curb Miriam's criticism. I'm grateful that God doesn't punish us with such powerful punishment or we would all be white with leprosy or much worse. Because Miriam was a woman of leadership and influence, I'm sure God wanted to nip this negativity in the bud and not allow it to continue. The message is clear—God is not pleased with a critical spirit, especially toward the one God had clearly put into place as the leader of Israel. God even asks Miriam why she was not afraid of criticizing him. Perhaps we need to ask ourselves the same question, why are we not afraid to be negative and critical of others?

> When Aaron saw what had happened to her, he cried out to Moses, "Oh, my master! Please don't punish us for this sin we have so foolishly committed. Don't let her be like a stillborn baby, already decayed at birth."
> So Moses cried out to the Lord, "O God, I beg you, please heal her!" [3]

Isn't this interesting? Now Moses is using his words to pray for his accuser! It reminds me of Jesus' words to "love your enemies, do good to those who hate you, bless those who curse you, pray for those who mistreat you."[4]

Lest we think that our critical tongues are not a big deal to God— let's think again! As I considered this story in my own heart, I thought about the times I have casually criticized someone in authority, or for that matter even an acquaintance of someone close to me. This story makes me want to shut my trap—and fast. God is serious about how we use our mouths. Solomon wrote, "The soothing tongue is a tree of life, but a perverse tongue crushes the spirit."[5] Let us not be spirit-crushers, but rather life-givers with our tongues.

Constructive Criticism or Critical Spirit?

Granted, constructive criticism and wise concern have their place. I'm not saying we ought to be some sort of "yes-people," who always agree with everyone about everything with disingenuous flattery. A true encourager is not only uplifting—she is also honest, sincere, and specific with her comments. She uses her words to help build up and lead others in the direction of their best interest. An encourager is looking out for the good of the other individual and focusing on the possibilities instead of hunting for and pecking at what could go wrong and zapping the hope right out of a person. A wise encourager looks with discernment for the solid stepping-stones to help a person walk forward into the future, without giving false hope or unrealistic expectations.

Let's use our opportunities to critique with a judicious sense of caution. How do you know when it is the right time to share a concern or a dissenting opinion? The best way to discern if your criticism is worth voicing is to ask yourself, *Will my comments essentially work for the betterment of the individual and the situation?* Constructive criticism possesses at its very core a desire to create positive change, building others up rather than tearing them down.

Bottom line, we must look at our motivation before we spill out negative appraisals or derogatory comments. Jealousy, envy, and rivalry are often the ugly, hidden motivations of a critical spirit. The queen of critique can harm hearts, reputations, and opportunities when she spews her poisonous venom. May God help each one of us examine the deep and hidden motives in our hearts and take the log out of our own eye before trying to remove the splinter from someone else's.

Worries and fears, and focusing on the negative outcomes, can also quickly turn us into Debbie Downers and Nancy Negatives. These women tend to cause defeat in others' lives before the game even starts because they feel it is their duty to save people from making mistakes or going down difficult roads. But what if we let people follow their dreams and make a few mistakes in the process? Then haven't they learned and grown in the process?

Let's not be a discouraging voice just because we are afraid of what may happen. Yes, there is a delicate balance between helping someone see the potholes and discouraging their dreams altogether. There is no perfect answer to the situation. The most important piece of advice I can give you is to *wait* before you point out a negative. I have found it helpful to do this: Before I allow myself to make a negative comment (intended to help the other person see the problems, of course), I wait. Often I wait several days in order to see if the situation has worked itself out. And most of the time I never need to say anything!

Criticizing people behind their backs is never helpful and is a big red flag that our motivation is not pure. Discretion and discernment are the traits of a wise person who uses their ability to assess an individual, situation, or idea with guarded reproof. On the other hand, the constant dripping of condemnation from a faultfinding friend can cause disunity, generating a negative environment—whether in a family, a neighborhood, or the workplace.

If you must offer a critique, always do it in the spirit of helpfulness and strength. Begin by praising what you see that is right in the person or situation, then carefully open up a broader perspective. Use words like "Have you thought about it this way?" or "Would it be possible to…?" Such phrases help the recipient take in your thought without feeling ridiculed or discouraged. Whenever you must relay a negative evaluation, try to offer positive alternatives as well.

Tongue-Tamer

It is never too late to change our speech habits. First, recognize the discouraging remarks that tend to flow out of your mouth, and then begin to guard your lips from the disparaging comments. Look for opportunities to give a good, sincere word of hope and courage. Think of your uplifting comments as a cup of cool water to a thirsty soul, because we all need a healthy dose of encouragement now and then. Don't become frustrated with yourself in the struggle to tame your tongue. In fact, the Bible speaks of its impossibility. James wrote, "All kinds of animals, birds, reptiles and sea creatures are being tamed and have been tamed by mankind, but no human being can tame the tongue. It is a restless evil, full of deadly poison."[6] Perhaps you are thinking that if the tongue is impossible to tame, then why try? What's the use?

Remember, my friend, with God all things are possible! What may seem impossible to us is not impossible for God. We know that He places great value on what comes out of our mouths, so He will help us in taming that restless creature known as the tongue. It begins by asking Him to clean up our hearts, for what comes out of our mouth is usually an overflow of what is in our heart. Our prayer ought to resemble that of David, who wrote, "May the words of my mouth and the meditation of my heart be pleasing to you, O Lord, my rock and my redeemer."[7] The Lord is our tongue-tamer. As we look to Him to clean us up from the inside out, He can clean up the hidden motives that tend to make us discouragers rather than encouragers.

⤜⦾⤛

Hatred, bitterness, jealousy, envy, fear, and fretting are not from God. The fruit of His Spirit in us is love, joy, peace, patience, kindness, goodness, faithfulness, gentleness, and self-control. These are the qualities that make us beautiful as women and give strength to our words. Kind and encouraging words cost so little, yet they are filled with riches and treasure of great worth. Be wealthy and generous with words of value, and enrich the world around you.

POWERFUL TRUTH

Our words can be used to build up and strengthen others, but they can also be used to hurt and destroy.

PLAN OF ACTION

1. Examine the type of comments you make to others. Are they encouraging or discouraging?

2. Evaluate your motives before you give a critique of any sort.

3. Never criticize someone behind their back.

4. Daily confess your critical words and ask God to help you guard your mouth.

5. Actively look for ways to build up others with sincerity and truth.

6. Recognize the power of your words and use them for good.

PAY IT FORWARD

Who do you know who needs an encouraging word? Maybe it is a leader, a teacher, a manager, a politician, or a neighbor. Consider a family member who may need a kind and uplifting word, beginning with your spouse and kids. Take the time to give them a word of sincere encouragement by phone, e-mail, a written note, or some other way. Make it an ongoing habit to deliberately reach out and encourage someone each week.

Place It in Your Heart

The soothing tongue is a tree of life,
but a perverse tongue crushes the spirit.

Proverbs 15:4

Discussion Starters

- Why is the tongue so difficult to tame?

- How have you found a balance between constructive and destructive criticism?

Chapter Five

Face Your Fears

Courage faces fear and thereby masters it.
Cowardice represses fear and is thereby mastered by it.

MARTIN LUTHER KING JR.

I sought the LORD, and he answered me;
he delivered me from all my fears.

PSALM 34:4

Sadly, I was the main source of entertainment in my junior-high French class. It was a role I didn't sign up for—it just happened. You see, as a blonde-haired, fair-skinned girl I had a face that turned the brightest, most peculiar shades of red you have ever seen when I was supposed to speak in front of the other students. French class gave me more than a fair share of opportunities to stand in front of class and recite passages or give a speech. Boys laughed at me and called me "Red" as I walked down the hall after class. You can imagine it was incredibly painful for me to even think about showing up for class, much less having to say anything in front of my classmates.

Now, 40 years later, I speak in front of men and women as part of my profession—go figure! How did I get here...from being that fearful little girl who prayed that God would send a snowstorm so I wouldn't have to go to class (that's pretty big faith—praying for a snowstorm when you live in Dallas, Texas) to now speaking in front of large audiences? Eventually, faith is what it took for me to face my fears and begin speaking in front of audiences. I began changing my focus and thinking about the message God had given me to deliver to the audience, rather than dwelling on what the audience was thinking about me. When it comes to the list of fears people commonly have, public speaking is one of the fears at the top of the list.

Facing an audience of people is one thing, but risking your life in facing the audience of a king is another. That's the fear Queen Esther had to face as she approached the king (uninvited) in order to save the lives of her people.

Esther offers us a powerful picture of a woman who faced her fears in a wise and intentional way. We all have fears, but the question is, what will we do with them? Will we allow our fears to take over our thinking, our lives, and our relationships? Or will we use them as an opportunity to trust God and move forward in courage and strength? Let's take a look at the example Esther provides from her slightly imperfect life.

A Time for Courage

Orphaned at an early age, young Esther was raised by her cousin Mordecai. She lived in the land of Persia in approximately 470 BC during the reign of King Xerxes. As exiled Jews in a foreign land, her people's future was unpredictable.

The king himself was a rather unpredictable guy. One time he held a grand banquet with all of the military leaders from Persia and Media. Princes and nobles from the provinces were all in attendance. The event went on for almost half a year, with lots of bragging and drinking and celebrating. One night the king decided to invite his wife, Queen Vashti, to parade around for everyone to observe her beauty. When she refused to come, the king became very angry and had no other choice but to dethrone her and search for a new queen.

A beauty contest to beat all beauty contests was held to find the next queen. Many women were brought before King Xerxes, including Esther. God allowed Esther to capture the heart of the king, and she soon became Queen Esther. But even being a queen had its limits. No one could approach the king's throne unless they had been summoned by him, not even the queen herself.

Meanwhile an enemy to the Jews named Haman rose in power in the king's court. In an interesting turn of events, Haman grew to despise Mordecai because he wouldn't bow down to him. As a result, Haman petitioned the king to have the Jews destroyed. Esther had kept her Jewish heritage a secret until this point—but now there was a decree proclaiming that the Jews were to be annihilated.

Mordecai sent a message to Esther in the palace alerting her to the situation and telling her to go before the king and plead for mercy. Now here's where we begin to get an inkling of the fear she was about to face. She replied to Mordecai, "All the king's officials and the people of the royal provinces know that for any man or woman who approaches the king in the inner court without being summoned the king has but one law: that they be put to death unless the king extends the gold scepter to them and spares their lives. But thirty days have passed since I was called to go to the king."[1]

Mordecai reminded her, "Do not think that because you are in the king's house you alone of all the Jews will escape. For if you remain silent at this time, relief and deliverance for the Jews will arise from another place, but you and your father's family will perish. And who knows but that you have come to your royal position for such a time as this?"[2] Mordecai trusted God and knew that God's timing was perfectly designed. Esther was in the palace for a purpose.

Courageously, Esther responded, "Go, gather together all the Jews who are in Susa, and fast for me. Do not eat or drink for three days, night or day. I and my attendants will fast as you do. When this is done, I will go to the king, even though it is against the law. And if I perish, I perish."[3]

"If I perish, I perish"! Now there's a woman who was willing to face her fears. But notice, she didn't move ahead with a plan until she had sought the Lord's direction and help. She didn't just ask everyone else to pray—she too diligently fasted and prayed.

Courage with Wisdom

Esther devised a very wise plan. She did not run in and face the dangerous situation haphazardly. No, she carefully prepared. I tend to believe that as she came before the Lord with her petition, He granted her wisdom in how to proceed in this delicate matter.

Here is a great lesson for all of us. As we face frightening situations, we can go to our wonderful and generous heavenly Father and seek His counsel and advice. He gives us not only comfort and courage, but He also gives us wisdom. I'm reminded of what we read from James:

> Consider it pure joy, my brothers and sisters, whenever you face trials of many kinds, because you know that the testing of your faith produces perseverance. Let perseverance finish its work so that you may be mature and complete, not lacking anything. If any of you lacks wisdom, you should ask God, who gives generously to all without finding fault, and it will be given to you. But when you ask, you must believe and not doubt,

because the one who doubts is like a wave of the sea, blown and tossed by the wind. That person should not expect to receive anything from the Lord. Such a person is double-minded and unstable in all they do.[4]

Esther did not simply rush in and demand that the Jews be saved. Fools rush in, but wise and courageous women carry out a plan of action. Esther prepared. After three days of praying, she put on her royal robes and stood in the inner court of the palace in front of the king's hall. The king was sitting on his royal throne in the hall facing the entrance, and when his eyes fell on the queen he was pleased and held out his golden scepter. He also offered to give her up to half the kingdom.

This is where I would have jumped ahead and said, "Please save my people! We are about to be killed." Yet in her guarded and patient wisdom, Esther simply asked for the king and Haman to come to a banquet. The king enjoyed the banquet so much he again offered her half the kingdom, but she graciously and patiently invited him and Haman to another banquet. Notice the patience she displayed in the middle of a tense time. She had given her cares to God, and she knew He was in control. Her faith was in Him, and her patience grew as a result.

Esther's story is one of the most faith-building stories in the Bible to me because we see here that God is in the details. David reminds us that God delights in the details of our lives, and this truth becomes obvious in the book of Esther. I want to encourage you to read this entire book of the Bible if you haven't already. Your heart will be moved by God's perfect orchestration of timing and events. If anything can soothe our fears, recognizing God's sovereignty will surely bring a beautiful calm to your anxious heart. He moved mightily in Xerxes' heart, and the tables were turned so that eventually Haman was hung on the gallows he had prepared for Mordecai. The Jews were also empowered to defend themselves. And everyone lived happily ever after…except for Haman and his family.

Esther knew the stakes were high, so she carefully prayed, planned, and prepared to face her fearful situation. Her patience and graciousness demonstrated that in the midst of fear, faith in God prevails. Queen Esther's slightly imperfect life gives us the opportunity to learn how to face our fears with wisdom and strength. Fears can pop into our heads and into our lives in the most surprising and unrelenting ways, but we don't have to be a slave to our fears. We can look to the Lord for courage every step of the way.

I am reminded of what Bethany Hamilton said about courage. "Courage doesn't mean you don't get afraid—courage means you don't let fear stop you." As you may remember, Bethany was the teen surfer in Hawaii who was attacked by a shark and lost an arm, yet she went on to compete in international surfing competitions. She faced her fears instead of letting them hold her back. Like Esther, she moved forward despite her fears.

Our Encourager

God is in the courage-giving business. Throughout the Bible we hear the call again and again: "Fear not, for I am with you." God's message is one of faith and courage, not fear and trembling. From Abraham to Joshua to Mary to the shepherds in the field on the night of Jesus' birth, God has been proclaiming to the generations, "Do not be afraid." In the psalms we are reminded, "Even when I walk through the darkest valley, I will not be afraid, for you are close beside me. Your rod and your staff protect and comfort me."[5] There is comfort in knowing we are not alone, that God is close beside us through our difficulties. What a reassurance comes when we remember His voice saying, "I am with you."

I'm reminded of the encouragement God gave Joshua as he took over the leadership of the Israelites:

> Keep this Book of the Law always on your lips; meditate on it day and night, so that you may be careful to do everything written in it. Then you will be prosperous and successful. Have I not commanded you? Be strong and courageous. Do not be afraid; do not be discouraged, for the LORD your God will be with you wherever you go.[6]

God wanted Joshua to continually meditate on His commands and to walk in courage. The Israelite leader had to face many difficult battles, but God gave him what he needed for each one. God doesn't want us to live in the discouragement of fear, but rather the courage of knowing He is with us.

Unhealthy Fears

Certain kinds of fear serve as a protection of sorts. For instance, we lock our doors for fear that someone may break in and steal from us. We use backup systems for our computers for fear of a virus or a computer crash, which would leave us without our documents and information. We purchase life insurance for fear that our families would face severe financial loss if something were to happen to us.

Certainly healthy fears help steer us away from destruction. In fact Solomon said, "The fear of the LORD is the beginning of wisdom."[7]

But an unhealthy fear of the what-ifs in life can grip us with anxiety and worry and can be unproductive and destructive in our lives. Unrelenting anxieties can lead to all sorts of physical disorders, not to mention relationship issues. Many of the arguments and disputes we have with others are based on some sort of fear of what could happen. Unhealthy fears can sometimes keep us from taking positive steps forward and moving toward our dreams.

In the writing world, there are many people who would love to have a book published one day, but they have never sent their book proposal to a publisher. Why? Fear of rejection. Fear of someone not liking their work. This fear keeps them locked in a box and trapped in chains of never living out their dreams.

Fears can rattle our thinking and take over our lives if we allow them to. What are you afraid of? Is it fear of something that may happen in the future? Are you unduly concerned about a job you must do or a test you must take? Perhaps you are afraid something may happen to you physically or financially—or in a relationship. As followers of Christ, we have a place we can take our fears. The invitation is open. God invites us to cast our cares and concerns on Him.

The God of peace wants to give us peace as we face those things that distress us. Our everlasting Father, God Almighty, is able to free us from the grip that fear has on our lives. He will never leave us, and He has a plan that is much bigger than what we can see. He can protect our reputations. He can use our mistakes. He will walk with us through difficulties. He redeems our lives from the pit. We must take our eyes off of what is worrying us, and turn them instead to His faithfulness. We can follow Esther's plan in facing her fears as she took those fears first to her heavenly Father. Then she wisely walked through a careful and deliberate plan of action. May God lead us each day as we turn our fears over to Him and allow our faith and joy to grow in their place.

I have found that praising God in the midst of my fears can transfer my focus from dread to delight—delighting in the Lord. I learned this life lesson from the apostle Paul, who praised God and prayed right in the deepest, darkest dungeon. When I choose to focus on the greatness and goodness of God, it helps me through the storms and reminds me that I am in good hands. He who is able to calm the storms of the sea can bring calm to my anxious heart as well. Praising Him strengthens our faith and turns our thinking toward His greatness, rather than the seeming bigness of our problems.

Facing your fears can be the very catalyst that moves you forward in your career or in your relationships. As we learn to walk forward without the shackles of worry and anxiety, we can step into new territory and grow in confidence and strength. Fears may pop into our heads now and then, but we don't need to allow them to get the best of us. We can change our focus and look upward.

Sure, it's tempting to take our fears to people first instead of the Lord. Who do you lean on for help? Do you lean on others, or even your own abilities and strengths—or do you lean on the Lord God Almighty (El-Shaddai)? He is mighty to save!

Take Your "Overwhelmed" Under Him

There can be times in life when the battle seems so large that we can't possibly imagine victory. Perhaps you are facing the fear of life after a divorce or living with a debilitating illness or dealing with a rebellious child or trying to make ends meet after losing a job. Fear of the unknown can also grip us and lead us into despair if we allow it.

The story of an Old Testament king comes to mind. Good King Jehoshaphat was king of Judah in the years around 850 BC. The Bible tells us his powerful story of facing seemingly insurmountable odds. Yet instead of letting himself be overcome by fear and despair, Jehoshaphat took his overwhelming circumstances and went straight to the Lord for help and counsel, just as Esther did. He took his "overwhelmed" and placed it under Him! Here's the dramatic story, which we can apply to our lives as well:

> Some people came and told Jehoshaphat, "A vast army is coming against you from Edom, from the other side of the Dead Sea. It is already in Hazezon Tamar" (that is, En Gedi). Alarmed, Jehoshaphat resolved to inquire of the LORD, and he proclaimed a fast for all Judah. The people of Judah came together to seek help from the LORD; indeed, they came from every town in Judah to seek him.[8]

Notice that Jehoshaphat was alarmed, but he didn't allow those thoughts to grip him. Instead he went directly to the Lord and told everyone else to do the same. He came to the Lord seeking wisdom and help, but notice how he started—by praising Him and recognizing all He had already done for the Israelites. Read on:

> Then Jehoshaphat stood up in the assembly of Judah and Jerusalem at the temple of the LORD in the front of the new courtyard and said: "LORD, the God of our

ancestors, are you not the God who is in heaven? You rule over all the kingdoms of the nations. Power and might are in your hand, and no one can withstand you. Our God, did you not drive out the inhabitants of this land before your people Israel and give it forever to the descendants of Abraham your friend? They have lived in it and have built in it a sanctuary for your Name, saying, 'If calamity comes upon us, whether the sword of judgment, or plague or famine, we will stand in your presence before this temple that bears your Name and will cry out to you in our distress, and you will hear us and save us.'

"But now here are men from Ammon, Moab and Mount Seir, whose territory you would not allow Israel to invade when they came from Egypt; so they turned away from them and did not destroy them. See how they are repaying us by coming to drive us out of the possession you gave us as an inheritance. Our God, will you not judge them? For we have no power to face this vast army that is attacking us. We do not know what to do, but our eyes are on you."[9]

Jehoshaphat recognized his great need. He admitted his powerlessness to face such a great army on his own, but his eyes were on the Lord.

When you feel overwhelmed or afraid, where are your eyes? What an important lesson to remember—take your eyes off of what is causing you fear and turn them instead toward the powerful and all-knowing God. I love Jehoshaphat's statement, "We do not know what to do, but our eyes are on you." That can be our continual prayer as well when we face battles or fears or worries. This would be a great phrase to memorize as we trust in our all-wise and loving heavenly Father.

> All the men of Judah, with their wives and children and little ones, stood there before the LORD. Then the Spirit of the LORD came on Jahaziel…as he stood in the assembly. He said: "Listen, King Jehoshaphat and all who live in Judah and Jerusalem! This is what the LORD says to you: 'Do not be afraid or discouraged because of this vast army. For the battle is not yours, but God's. Tomorrow march down against them. They will be climbing up by the Pass of Ziz, and you will find them at the end of the gorge in the Desert of Jeruel. You will not have to fight this battle. Take up your positions; stand firm and see the deliverance the LORD will give you, Judah and Jerusalem. Do not be afraid; do not be discouraged. Go out to face them tomorrow, and the LORD will be with you.'"[10]

Following God's Wisdom

God gave the Israelites clear instructions and they followed them. They didn't do what they wanted to do (which was probably to run)— they did what He called them to do. They asked for wisdom in the midst of danger, and He guided them. It is interesting to me that they didn't ask for the problem to just go away. Instead they sought God's direction and help to face the challenge. God may not remove our tough or fearful situation, but He is generous with wisdom and guidance in maneuvering through our difficulties.

Jehoshaphat bowed down with his face to the ground, and all the people of Judah and Jerusalem fell down in worship before the Lord. Then some Levites from the Kohathites and Korahites stood up and praised the Lord, the God of Israel, with a very loud voice.[11]

They began praising God for His direction and care. They had not yet experienced the victory, but they praised Him nonetheless. This again reminds me of Paul and Silas praying and praising God right in the deepest, darkest prison, having just been severely beaten. They praised Him even before they saw the answer to their prayers. In the middle of our fear and anxieties, let us praise the Lord! It changes our perspective and increases our faith. Now let's see how God fought the battle for Jehoshaphat:

Early in the morning they left for the Desert of Tekoa. As they set out, Jehoshaphat stood and said, "Listen to me, Judah and people of Jerusalem! Have faith in the Lord your God and you will be upheld; have faith in his prophets and you will be successful." After consulting the people, Jehoshaphat appointed men to sing to the Lord and to praise him for the splendor of his holiness as they went out at the head of the army, saying: "Give thanks to the Lord, for his love endures forever."

As they began to sing and praise, the Lord set ambushes against the men of Ammon and Moab and Mount Seir who were invading Judah, and they were defeated. The Ammonites and Moabites rose up against the men from Mount Seir to destroy and annihilate them. After they finished slaughtering the men from Seir, they helped to destroy one another.[12]

God fought their battle for them as they followed His direction. Although the details were different, both Esther and Jehoshaphat faced their fears by turning their eyes toward the Lord. He fought their battle for them.

❧

Three practical applications come to mind from these examples of faith at the door of fear: Seek God's help and direction, praise Him in the midst of your challenge, and remember the battle is the Lord's. Just as Esther and Jehoshaphat asked others to join with them in prayer, surround yourself with people who can pray for you as you face the battles ahead. Do not be discouraged, and do not give in to despair, my friend. Instead, face your fear with courage as you put your eyes on God and take them off your circumstances.

Positive Life Strategy

Powerful Truth

We can replace our fears with faith in God
and with seeking His wisdom and direction.

Plan of Action

1. Recognize the fears that lurk in your life.

2. Seek God's direction and help.

3. Praise and thank Him in the midst of your worries and fears.

4. Remember the battle is the Lord's.

5. Do not be discouraged and do not give in to despair.

6. Ask for His peace, which passes all understanding.

7. Walk forward with wisdom, patience, and faith.

Pay It Forward

Help someone who is dealing with fear or worry about a circumstance in their life (perhaps a financial loss, a wayward child, a divorce, or a physical challenge) and offer to support them in prayer. Encourage their faith and reassure them that the Lord is close to the brokenhearted and walks with us through our darkest valleys. Just as Esther had the support of other Jews joining together with her in prayer and fasting as she faced her fear, let us be a spiritual support to others with our prayers and words of hope and encouragement. We all need a personal prayer warrior at times.

Place It in Your Heart

Cast your cares on the Lord and he will sustain you.

Psalm 55:22

Discussion Starters

• What is your first inclination to do when you are afraid?

• Why do you think God does not want us to be consumed by our fears?

Chapter Six
Reach Out and Help Others

*By compassion we make others' misery our own,
and so, by relieving them, we relieve ourselves also.*

Sir Thomas Browne

*As God's chosen people, holy and
dearly loved, clothe yourselves
with compassion, kindness, humility,
gentleness and patience.*

Colossians 3:12

If given the opportunity to choose our path in life, I'm pretty sure most of us would pick the easier road—the one with fewer bumps, potholes, and challenges. Few of us would deliberately choose a difficult journey in life, riddled with heartache, pain, and loss. Yet in a way, if we choose to be compassionate people, we are choosing to join ourselves to someone else's pain. The word *compassion* actually means "with-suffering." The root word, *passion*, comes from the Latin word *passio*, meaning "suffering." If we want to be a compassionate person, then we are inviting suffering into our lives—the suffering of another person. How far are we willing to go to reach out and touch the life of someone else, joining in their pain?

It's easy to sign up to sponsor an orphan child in India, write our monthly check, and stay at a distance. And yes, we do need to reach out in this way. Since God has blessed us with so much, we can joyfully give to those who have nothing.[1] Writing a check for someone in need or going on a mission trip is certainly an important way to show compassion abroad, but sometimes it is easy to overlook the more difficult acts of compassion right in front of us. Are we willing to roll up our sleeves and help serve those closest to us?

Mother Teresa, whose love reached around the world, said, "I want you to be concerned about your next-door neighbor. Do you know your next-door neighbor?" In other words, we can be concerned about the people across the globe, but what about the person God has placed next to us? Are we willing to step out of our comfort zone and touch someone close to us with loving-kindness and compassion?

❧

I remember one mission-trip leader telling me that it was easier for him to go on a one-week mission trip around the world than to reach out to neighbors and those closest to him. Let's go ahead and admit it—it's difficult to care for the ongoing needs of a friend or neighbor whom we will see again and again. It's possible they may inconvenience us and disrupt our normal lifestyle, as some of them may continue to need us for a long time. (To be sure, there is wisdom in setting boundaries, because there are certain people who will take advantage of your availability and become dependent in an unhealthy way.)

Can I be honest with you? I often hesitate to reach out to those closest to me because of the fear they will demand ongoing time and attention. An ongoing commitment tends to make me feel straitjacketed. Have you ever felt that way? Did you notice something in my last statement? Did you pick up on the word *fear*? Wait a minute—didn't we just address the issue of fear in the last chapter? Perhaps showing compassion to those closest to us demands a bit of facing our fears—specifically the fear that we will be "imprisoned" by a needy person for an unknown period of time.

If we apply what we learned in the last chapter, then we ought to pray and seek the Lord's guidance on how we can best show compassion to others in need. We can also pray for the Lord to give us wisdom in setting wise boundaries so that we guard against being an enabler. Our goal is to truly help, encourage, and elevate our neighbors, friends, or family members in need, and the Lord can lead us in how to do that in a wise and meaningful way. The Bible describes God as compassionate and gracious; His very nature is love. He will give us the direction we need as we desire to reach out to others in compassion and love, whether they are close by or on the other side of the world.

Just another word here on the importance of boundaries. As we talk about reaching out in compassion we must also recognize that we are not everybody's savior. Sometimes we must allow people to take ownership of their challenges, helping them recognize their need to carry their own load and trust God for their direction and strength rather than putting all their dependence on people.*

---

* If you struggle with finding a balance between compassion and enabling, I recommend two great books on setting boundaries: *Setting Boundaries with Difficult People* by Allison Bottke (Harvest House Publishers, 2011), and *Boundaries* by Henry Cloud and John Townsend (Zondervan Publishing, 1992).

Wonderfully Willing

There is one stellar example of a woman who reached out with true compassion in the Old Testament. Ruth did not choose the easy road of "You deal with your issues, I'll deal with mine." No, instead she chose the narrower path, the road less traveled, the road of "I'll join in with you and help you carry your burden." Her kindness creates a portrait of patient love and enduring dedication, which serves to inspire all of us to die to self and live with outstretched arms. Her life had its own set of challenges, yet she did not allow her own difficulties to develop into an opportunity to make excuses.

As we consider the slightly imperfect life of Ruth, we must begin by looking at her heritage. Ruth was a Moabite woman. Now you may say to yourself, *Who cares? Does that really matter?* It did matter if you were a Jew. There was long-standing hostility between the Moabites and Israelites. Located just east of the Dead Sea, Moab was one of the nations that oppressed Israel during the period of the judges. Friendly relations with them were discouraged, and marriage between the Jews and the Moabites was forbidden. A person of Moabite descent was not allowed to worship at the tabernacle, because of a long-standing grievance going back to the days when the Israelites were journeying through the wilderness. The Moabites had denied the Israelites the right to pass through their land during the exodus from Egypt. Sounds like the Hatfields and McCoys or perhaps the Montagues and the Capulets, doesn't it?

Now there was a certain Israelite who lived in Bethlehem, named Elimelech, who took his wife, Naomi, and his two sons to go live in the land of Moab during a time of famine. It must have been a pretty bad famine if he moved into Moabite territory! While they were there, Elimelech died, so Naomi stayed on in Moab with her sons. As you may have guessed, the two sons married Moabite women, but after about ten years, the boys also died. Naomi had not only lost her husband, but she had also lost her sons. Widows in the ancient world were often ignored and poverty-stricken in society. Naomi had little hope in a foreign land, yet she had heard that the famine had subsided in Israel, and she decided to make the journey to return to her homeland. God's law provided that the nearest relative of the dead husband should take care of the widow, so perhaps she thought she could find help there.

On the road home, Naomi told her daughters-in-law to go back to their families and start a fresh new life there. This was big decision time for the two younger women! Two paths. One path led to the comfort and security of their own people and family along with the possibility of starting over with a new husband. The other path meant caring for a depressed mother-in-law while facing hostility as a Moabite in Israel territory—and no guarantee of remarriage. Tough decision: comfort and security versus sharing in someone else's suffering and insecure future. Which path would you choose?

One of the daughters-in-law, named Ruth, chose the high road, the road less traveled, the road that was paved with love but that required commitment and dying to self. Perhaps you are familiar with her words of kindness:

> Don't urge me to leave you or to turn back from you.
> Where you go I will go, and where you stay I will stay.
> Your people will be my people and your God my God.
> Where you die I will die, and there I will be buried. May

the Lord deal with me, be it ever so severely, if even death separates you and me.[2]

Ruth didn't just love with her words, she loved with her actions. She reached out to a woman who needed her help, and she dedicated herself to sticking in there for the long run.

Reaching Out to Opportunity

But this was only the beginning of Ruth's story. God shined His favor upon this kind woman who demonstrated love in action toward her mother-in-law. Ruth became quite adept at stepping out of her comfort zone and reaching out to opportunity. She needed to gather food for Naomi and herself, so she went and collected the leftover wheat from a field owned by one of Naomi's distant relatives, named Boaz. Boaz was aware of Ruth's reputation—in fact her compassionate character was the talk of the town. When he first met her, he said, "I've been told all about what you have done for your mother-in-law since the death of your husband—how you left your father and mother and your homeland and came to live with a people you did not know before. May the Lord repay you for what you have done. May you be richly rewarded by the Lord, the God of Israel, under whose wings you have come to take refuge."[3]

Don't miss the beauty of what Boaz said. Not only did Ruth's acts of compassion reveal the beauty of her heart, but they also demonstrated her spiritual source of strength. Notice how marvelously Boaz put it: "The God of Israel, under whose wings you have come to take refuge." We saw this reflected in Ruth's initial pledge to Naomi. She not only chose to help, but she chose the God of Israel as her God. She stepped away from the pagan gods of her heritage and through faith believed in the one true God. Under His wings she found her refuge and her strength. What about you? Could it be said of you what was said of Ruth? Have you come to take refuge under His mighty and powerful wings? Perhaps this is what enabled Ruth to spread her wings and fly—knowing that she was cared for by a compassionate and loving God.

I'm reminded of David's words describing the love and care of the Lord:

> Your love, LORD, reaches to the heavens,
> > your faithfulness to the skies.
> Your righteousness is like the highest mountains,
> > your justice like the great deep.
> > You, LORD, preserve both people and animals.
> How priceless is your unfailing love, O God!
> > People take refuge in the shadow of your wings.
> They feast on the abundance of your house;
> > you give them drink from your river of delights.
> For with you is the fountain of life;
> > in your light we see light.[4]

When Naomi found out that Ruth had been to Boaz's field, she encouraged her to reach out to Boaz as their "kinsman redeemer." A *kinsman redeemer* was a relative who was required to take responsibility for a widow in the family.[5] Ruth followed her mother-in-law's advice and went to the threshing floor to request Boaz's covering as her kinsman redeemer.

Here's another example of Ruth reaching out beyond her comfort zone. And what a happy ending her story had! Eventually she and Boaz were married and had a son named Obed. And in God's

---

wonderful design, Obed was the father of Jesse, and Jesse was the father of King David!

God Reaches Out in Compassion

Ruth's story is a snapshot of a much bigger and grander story of compassion; a story which includes redemption and grace at the very center of the stage. Think about how God in His grace chose to use a despised Moabite woman to be a part of the lineage of King David and eventually Jesus. He didn't use someone who seemed to have the perfect life or a qualified background. He used Ruth, a foreigner and a widow, whose status was among the lowest in society. She was an unlikely character in the beautiful plan of redemption, but that's what grace is all about. God in His graciousness and compassion reached past the hostility and social status and elevated this woman to a place in the lineage of Christ.

God has always been in the compassion business. Because of His great compassion toward us, He reached down into this world full of sinners to save and redeem those who believe in Christ. He has kindly given us the right to be His very own children. God could have left us to die in our sin, but instead He took action—and it wasn't convenient. He sent His one and only Son to suffer and die on our behalf. The Bible tells us that in our relationships with one another, we are to

> have the same mindset as Christ Jesus: Who, being in very nature God, did not consider equality with God something to be used to his own advantage; rather, he made himself nothing by taking the very nature of a servant, being made in human likeness. And being

found in appearance as a man, he humbled himself by becoming obedient to death—even death on a cross!⁶

The Lord reached out in compassion toward us, and we ought also to reach out toward others. Christ was willing to leave the comfort of heaven in order to walk the road of suffering on our behalf. You have heard of the passion of Christ? Well, remember that passion (*passio*) means suffering. He suffered for us. He gave us the perfect picture of compassion in its deepest, richest sense when He chose to give His life on our behalf. "Greater love has no one than this: to lay down one's life for one's friends."⁷ Are we willing to lay aside our convenience and comfort in order to reach out to touch another person's life? Let's pray for God to open our eyes to the opportunities in our own backyard—our neighbors, our family members, our friends—as well as those around the world. Pray for wisdom about how to truly help those in need, and pray for the courage to put your love into action.

True compassion doesn't just give a handout—it elevates another person to help them become better. God didn't just stamp a "forgiven" label on us and then send us out to continue in bondage to sin—He chose to transform our lives. He gave us His Spirit to live inside us and help us live with love in action. He gave us the power to overcome sin and walk in His ways. As we reflect His compassion in this world, we too can consider how we can go beyond giving simply handouts. It's much more significant and long-lasting when we can give a hand *up*—a way to help those in need to experience dignity and hope. As we help with physical needs, let us also bring encouragement spiritually, for the gospel message brings lasting positive change to a person's life.

A True Gem

My friend Jewel is a true treasure. Although small in stature, she is a powerhouse of active compassion and gentle strength. Like Ruth, Jewel is a widow. When her husband passed away, it would have been easy for her to sit back and rest after the difficult years surrounding his death. But Jewel is not a woman who takes the easy road. Even before her husband's death she began reaching out to people in a variety of places in Eastern Europe through a local ministry that serves countries around the world. Weeks after her husband's death, she traveled to Uganda to minister to hundreds of women. She said she could have stayed home and cried, but instead she wanted to get up and go forward to bring hope to those women in Uganda. And she received the hugs of hundreds of women to help her through her grief.

Jewel's home is decorated with memories from the myriad of people she has met on mission trips around the world. In Nigeria, Sudan, and Uganda, Jewel began a wedding-dress ministry, giving away donated wedding dresses in order to elevate the women with beauty while teaching them the value of the marriage vows. She also loves to go to Peru, where she has an ongoing friendship with many people in the villages there. I can easily say that Jewel sparkles as she brings joy to people all over the world.

Additionally, she reaches out to people in her own community. I know Jewel because she serves as a table leader at my Positive Woman Connection Bible study, and she often brings visitors with her. She also helps and encourages a prisoner in a local jail, bringing Bible studies and encouragement to this person who needs a good word of hope. She blesses her family and takes them with her when she can on mission trips. In fact, as I write this chapter, she's on a mission trip with her granddaughter, visiting an Asian country that is normally closed to the gospel.

❦

Both Ruth and Jewel remind me of Proverbs 31, which is a memorable description of a woman of noble character: "She opens her arms to the poor and extends her hands to the needy…she is clothed with strength and dignity…'Many women do noble things, but you surpass them all.'"[8] The description goes on to say, "Charm is deceptive, and beauty is fleeting; but a woman who fears the LORD is to be praised. Honor her for all that her hands have done, and let her works bring her praise at the city gate."[9] Perhaps the writer was thinking about his own mother when he wrote this, but I also think he was describing women like Jewel who live beyond themselves to lift up others. What about you? Are you a Jewel?

Positive Life Strategy

POSITIVE TRUTH

Compassion means having the courage to step out of our comfort zone and reach out to share in someone else's suffering.

PLAN OF ACTION

1. Choose to take the tough road at times.

2. Reach out and help in a variety of ways, both near and far.

3. Look for opportunities to help those closest to you.

4. Ask God to lead you and guide you in serving wisely.

5. Don't just give a handout—give a hand up as well.

6. Let actions, not words, define your compassion.

Pay It Forward

Deliberately reach out of your comfort zone and look for someone in your immediate surroundings who needs a touch of compassion and care. Ask the Lord to lead you as to how to actively demonstrate God's love to that person and help them. Consider ways you can elevate them to a place where they can experience not only dignity, but lasting hope and transformation.

Place It in Your Heart

Dear children, let us not love with words or speech but with actions and in truth.

1 John 3:18

Discussion Starters

- What is the difference between a handout and a hand up?

- How can setting boundaries allow you more freedom to reach out? What kinds of boundaries make sense when you are reaching out to others?

Chapter Seven

Be Proactive Rather Than Reactive

*True spiritual self-discipline holds believers in bounds
but never in bonds;
its effect is to enlarge, expand and liberate.*

D.G. Kehl

*Never be lacking in zeal, but keep your
spiritual fervor, serving the Lord.
Be joyful in hope, patient in affliction, faithful in prayer.*

Romans 12:11-12

Have you ever been to one of those giant water parks? Recently I invited my college-age daughter and her friend to join me at a speaking engagement in Grapevine, Texas. I thought it would be fun to stay at a hotel with a large water park inside so they could entertain themselves while I went off and spoke. Now I want you to know this was no small place. In fact I would call it a Texas-sized park! Gigantic slides with all sorts of crazy twists and turns. I'd never seen anything like it. I was thrilled that my daughter and her friend would enjoy the rides, but I really had not planned on going on the slides myself. Well, at least not until my daughter talked me into it.

I must admit, the first few slides were not so bad. In fact they were rather exhilarating! I felt so young and vibrant conquering the twists and turns and waterfalls. Just when I thought I had had enough, my daughter talked me into going down one more slide. I should have known this was not a good thing when it took us almost 20 minutes to climb the stairs to the top of this ginormous slide.

I continued to assure myself that this would be fun—no problem, I could handle it. Everyone rode together in rafts on this particular ride, so how bad could it be? What I didn't know was that my daughter and her friend had already plotted to have me go down this scary slide backward. While I was getting into the raft, they secretly told the lifeguard to turn it so I would be going down with no advance warnings during the whole ride. Oh my! This was the most hair-raising slide I had ever been on. It had an actual giant funnel at its center, where you swish around and then slip through the middle! That part of the ride is nicknamed "The Toilet Bowl." Have you ever been flushed down a giant-size toilet bowl? Well, now I have! I want you to know it is a scary adventure, to say the least.

Once the ride was over, with my knees shaking I hobbled over to the Lazy River ride and told the kids to go off and play. In case you are wondering, I did forgive them—but only because that is what God tells us to do. As I plopped down on my nice, safe inner tube in the gentle current of the Lazy River, I was finally able to recuperate a bit. It was delightful. With the exception of a few pesky, splashing kids, it was total relaxation. I remember thinking to myself, *This is the life. This is what I want life to be like—calm, smooth, and predictable.* Then it hit me. Although I want life to be like a lazy river with predictable peace and serenity, life is more like the giant slide with twists and turns that we don't know are coming…some fun and some scary!

The question is not *if* any twists and turns will come into our lives. The real question is, *when* the unexpected twists and turns happen in our lives, how will we respond? We have a choice. We can choose to kick and scream the whole way through, or we can choose to respond with strength, remaining flexible and growing through the adventure. (I know how I want to respond, but I don't always do it.)

In our response, we can take a proactive stance or a reactive one. When we are proactive, we step back, observe the big picture, and consider the options in front of us. We remain flexible and look for opportunities. When we are reactive, our response usually erupts out of fear and impatience. When we react with negativity or anger to circumstances, we are often only focusing on what is right smack-dab in front of us rather than looking to the Lord and broadening our perspective so we can move forward with wisdom.

Averting Disaster

Most of us have a desire to respond respectfully and wisely rather than react foolishly when difficult circumstances come our way. But as much as we desire to respond with wisdom and collectedness, our emotional reaction can get the better of us. We find a story in the Old Testament brimming over with this contrast: one person who reacts foolishly and abruptly to his circumstances, while another responds with a calm, cool, and collected head about herself. We can learn a great deal about life and our responses as we take a peek into the home life of Abigail and Nabal.

Abigail demonstrated patience and understanding within her slightly imperfect marriage. In order to understand the challenges she faced in life, we must first meet her husband, Nabal. Although

Nabal was a very wealthy man, the Bible also tells us he was surly and mean in his dealings. He was wicked, short-tempered, and reactive. His name meant "fool," for folly went with him, as the Scripture tells us. Abigail, as his wife, knew all too well about the foolish actions of this angry man. Yet she seemed to respond with dignity and grace to circumstances despite her difficult husband. The Bible tells us that she was not only beautiful, but she was also intelligent. Their relationship truly could be labeled "Beauty and the Beast"!

Their story begins when David approaches Nabal's men with a request. David was well-known throughout the country for his slaying of Goliath and as a part of King Saul's court. But Saul had become jealous of David, and as a result the king was now hunting him down. David and his men moved from place to place and town to town in order to avoid him. They ended up in a desert near Nabal's fields.

David sent some of his men to greet Nabal with genuine, warm courtesy and to ask for some provisions. David's followers had been kind to Nabal's shepherds in the fields, and David hoped that Nabal would return the favor. But, instead of responding with wisdom and hospitality, cantankerous Nabal responded by saying, "Who is this David? Who is this son of Jesse? Many servants are breaking away from their masters these days. Why should I take my bread and water and meat I have slaughtered for my shearers, and give it to men coming from who knows where?"[1]

David didn't take Nabal's reaction too well. In fact, he was livid. He told his men (there were about 400 of them) to mount and get their swords. He was ready for battle, and he headed toward Nabal's house! One of the servants told Abigail what had happened. He warned her,

---

David sent messengers from the wilderness to give our master his greetings, but he hurled insults at them. Yet these men were very good to us. They did not mistreat us, and the whole time we were out in the fields near them nothing was missing. Night and day they were a wall around us the whole time we were herding our sheep near them. Now think it over and see what you can do, because disaster is hanging over our master and his whole household. He is such a wicked man that no one can talk to him.[2]

Planning, Not Panicking

Now here's where we see the beauty in Abigail's response. At this point she could have despaired and panicked, thinking their lives were over. She could have run in and yelled at Nabal, saying, "What were you thinking! Can't you see you've made David mad? You'd better retract your words before it's too late!" (although, over the years, she had probably learned that the "talk it out with Nabal" approach didn't ever work). She could have prepared the servants for battle to defend the home front, all the while complaining about her foolish husband who had once again put them into a terrible fix.

But she didn't do any of these things. Instead, she thoughtfully made a proactive plan. Time was of the essence, so she gathered 200 loaves of bread, 2 skins of wine, 5 dressed sheep, 5 bushels of grain, 100 cakes of raisins, and 200 cakes of pressed figs and loaded them on donkeys. Yes, she whipped into action. She sent her servants ahead of her and didn't tell Nabal where she was going. When she saw David, she quickly got off her donkey and bowed down before him with her face on the ground. What a picture of humility! What a contrast to Nabal's haughty pride! Next she carefully mediated the situation. She offered gifts and asked forgiveness for her husband's reaction. She appealed to David's ego and his conscience, knowing he was a man who feared God.

Her plan worked! Disaster was averted due to this brave woman's actions. Here's how David responded,

> "Praise be to the LORD, the God of Israel, who has sent you today to meet me. May you be blessed for your good judgment and for keeping me from bloodshed this day and from avenging myself with my own hands. Otherwise, as surely as the LORD, the God of Israel, lives, who has kept me from harming you, if you had not come quickly to meet me, not one male belonging to Nabal would have been left alive by daybreak."
>
> Then David accepted from her hand what she had brought him and said, "Go home in peace. I have heard your words and granted your request."[3]

Notice the vast difference between a man who feared God and one who did not. When David was presented with the whole picture, he wanted to do the right thing, for he feared God and wanted to obey Him. Nabal, on the other hand, had no fear of God. He did what he wanted and lived with a reckless attitude. Once again, we must reflect on Solomon's words: "The fear of the LORD is the beginning of wisdom." In David's speech we pick up a deep sense of reverence toward God. Not with Nabal! Fearing God keeps us from foolish reactions because we live with a sense of knowing we must ultimately answer to our heavenly Father.

A Woman of Vision

Abigail proved herself to be a woman of vision and faith. She didn't say, "Oh no!" in her precarious situation; she said, "Okay, let's make a plan!" She didn't focus on what she couldn't do—she looked for what she could do. One of the reasons she had a positive outlook is because she was a big-picture thinker. How do I know this? In her "power meeting" with David, her humble request for forgiveness was mixed with a positive and potent visionary statement. Here's what she said:

> Please forgive your servant's presumption. The Lord your God will certainly make a lasting dynasty for my lord, because you fight the Lord's battles, and no wrongdoing will be found in you as long as you live. Even though someone is pursuing you to take your life, the life of my lord will be bound securely in the bundle of the living by the Lord your God, but the lives of your enemies he will hurl away as from the pocket of a sling. When the Lord has fulfilled for my lord every good thing he promised concerning him and has appointed him ruler over Israel, my lord will not have on his conscience the staggering burden of needless bloodshed or of having avenged himself. And when the Lord your God has brought my lord success, remember your servant.[4]

Did you catch that? She knew beyond a shadow of a doubt that David was destined for the throne. She believed in God's plan, and she knew He would carry it out. Nabal in his shortsighted vision simply saw a bothersome bunch of men who just wanted his food.

Abigail saw the man who was going to be king and recognized the importance of having a peaceful and positive relationship with him. Her vision was for the future and the hope that David would remember her in his success. Notice that she continued to point to the Lord and His plan, taking the focus off the squabble with Nabal.

There is an interesting twist to the end of this story. When Nabal was told about what Abigail had done, his heart gave out and he died. Guess who sent for Abigail to be his bride! Yes, David was so impressed by her wisdom in handling the sticky situation that he wanted her for his wife. God honored her and blessed her wise actions and reverence for Him.

Strength Through Flexibility

A friend once told me, "A flexible woman rarely gets bent out of shape." I like that! Plans change, challenges arise, and mistakes happen. We must remain flexible in the process. A flexible woman looks for alternative plans and wise options. A flexible woman doesn't sit back and say, "This is the way we have always done it." She recognizes the opportunity to jump into action instead of stewing in anger or fear. An old Japanese proverb says, "The bamboo which bends is stronger than the oak that resists." Nabal was inflexible. He was stuck in his ways and shortsighted. Abigail, on the other hand, was flexible, responding to her challenges with grace and positive action.

How do we grow to be flexible in God's hands? It comes down to our beliefs. If we believe that God is sovereign and that He loves us, we can look to Him as the winds of change or challenge blow through our lives. Our faith changes the way we respond to circumstances. Knowing that He is the God who sees all keeps us from despair. We can respond to situations with the calm assurance that He will never leave us and that His hand will guide us. We can say to ourselves, "Although this is not what I planned, I can trust that God will bring something good out of the situation."

We can learn to be flexible and respond with grace when our eyes are on the Lord and our trust is in His plan. There are no guarantees about what tomorrow will bring, but we do know we are not alone in the battles we face. Like Abigail, we can put our faith into action and move forward to make a difference in a seemingly impossible situation. The following poem reminds us of the difference our faith makes in how we view our circumstances.

> My Father's way may twist and turn,
> My heart may throb and ache.
> But in my soul I'm glad I know,
> He maketh no mistake.
>
> My cherished plans may go astray,
> My hopes may fade away,
> But still I'll trust my Lord to lead,
> For He doth know the way.
>
> Tho' night be dark and it may seem
> That day will never break,
> I'll pin my faith, my all, in Him,
> He maketh no mistake.
>
> There's so much now I cannot see,
> My eyesight's far too dim,
> But come what may,
> I'll simply trust and leave it all to Him.

For by and by the mist will lift,
And plain it all He'll make,
Through all the way, tho' dark to me,
He made not one mistake![5]

—A.M. Overton

We can trust God's sovereign grace in whatever comes our way, and live with assurance that He will walk with us. We don't need to fret or complain, just advance with a humble trust in the God who loves us and has a big and beautiful plan. Step forward, my friend, with your eyes on Him—and your faith in the work He has yet to do in your life.

Positive Life Strategy

POWERFUL TRUTH

Through the twists and turns of life, respond with wisdom, faith, and action.

PLAN OF ACTION

1. Enrich your faith in God through reading His Word and prayer.

2. Stay flexible through the storms of life.

3. Keep your eyes on the bigger picture.

4. Don't waste time complaining or worrying.

5. Make a positive plan, keeping your eyes on God for direction and strength.

6. Look for what you can do, rather than focusing on what you can't get done.

7. Resolve issues with humility and kindness.

Pay It Forward

Is there someone to whom you need to make amends? Do you have a conflict with someone that needs to be resolved? Prayerfully make a plan to go to them and make things right. Reflect on Abigail's humble mediation with David. She not only built David up, but also asked for forgiveness. Most importantly, she continually pointed to the Lord and worked toward an amicable resolution.

Place It in Your Heart

Trust in the Lord with all your heart
    and lean not on your own understanding;
In all your ways submit to him,
    and he will make your paths straight.

Proverbs 3:5-6

Discussion Starters

- In what types of situations is it most difficult for you to respond with wisdom and graciousness?

- How can you be more proactive in your responses in the future?

Chapter Eight

Believe Big

*We are not to think that where we see no
possibility, God sees none.*

MARCUS DODS

*Now to him who is able to do immeasurably more than all
we ask or imagine, according to his
power that is at work within us,
to him be glory in the church and in Christ Jesus
throughout all generations, for ever and ever! Amen.*

EPHESIANS 3:20-21

Laura Glass often encourages her friends with the words, "You never know what is around the corner! God's plan is better than our plan." Indeed, Laura learned this lesson in her own life and now loves to help other women find hope despite their challenges. She says that what she thought was the worst day of her life actually turned out to be one of the best days of her life. The day her son, Billy Ray, was born, the doctors immediately informed Laura and her husband that their son might not live. Billy Ray not only had Down syndrome, but he also had a life-threatening obstruction in his stomach. But God had big plans for the Glass family and for Billy Ray!

At first, Laura struggled with the fact that life would be different in raising a Downs child. She didn't know what to expect, nor did she have an idea of what the future would hold for her son as he grew older. There were many days when she felt sad and blue as she struggled through this unexpected journey. Her husband, Billy, tried to help her accept her new normal and to let go of her old expectations of what life would be like. Progressively she grieved the loss of the old dream and began to embrace and appreciate what she did have. Billy encouraged her that she could make the choice every day to be happy.

Laura decided that as she got up from bed each morning and put her feet on the floor, she would tell herself, *Today is going to be a good day.* Gradually she made the turn from being sad to being glad for all that God had given her.

She began to realize she had underestimated what Billy Ray could do. He learned to ride a bike like his two brothers. It took a few years, but he eventually got there through persistence, help, and encouragement from his parents. He began participating in Special Olympics, and when a new swimming facility was built near their house, Laura decided to help several of the special athletes to learn how to swim. She started out with five. As the class size grew, she invited students from the local swim team to help teach the special swimmers.

Several other mothers who were looking for a way to do service work with their sons saw the wonderful opportunity, so they started an organization called SASO (Scholars and Athletes Serving Others). SASO took on the joyful responsibility of helping the special swimmers, and they organized swim meets in which the swimmers could compete. At one of their recent meets they had 200 athletes and 90 volunteers. Laura had no idea when she started with just five special needs swimmers that it would grow to this!

Billy Ray is currently a spokesperson for Special Olympics in their Global Messengers program, telling large audiences more about the organization. One of his greatest joys is going to church on Sunday morning and worshipping the Lord. He sings in the 9:30 a.m. service and attends the two other morning services as well! Laura and Billy said that everyone knows them as "Billy Ray's parents" because their son is so popular in the church and community. His favorite saying, which he tells everyone, is "Let God do the work!"

Billy Ray works at a grocery store and brings constant joy to the customers. Laura says, "With Down syndrome kids there is a whole lot of love going on." Billy Ray's love is the purest form of love, a God-type love. He shows others how to sincerely and genuinely reach out and encourage through love and kindness. Laura's smile says it all. She knows that God has done more than she could have ever dreamed through the blessing of Billy Ray, and she looks forward to all that God has in store for him. He is a big God with big plans, far beyond what we can ask or imagine. What about you? How big is your view of God?

Determination Through Difficulties

Armin Gesswein said, "When God is about to do something great, he starts with a difficulty. When he is about to do something truly magnificent, he starts with an impossibility."[1]

Often it is in the midst of difficulties that our faith grows and we lean in on God just a little more closely. Such was the case with the widow who approached Elisha with her troubles. The Bible tells us that she was the widow of a man from the company of the prophets, so most likely she was not a stranger to Elisha. The Bible doesn't give us her name, but it does tell us that she "cried out to Elisha," which implies desperation. Indeed she was desperate. Since her husband was dead, she was unable to pay off her debts, and now the creditor was coming to take her two sons as his slaves!

This wise woman knew her need, but more important, she knew who to cry out to. She was well aware of Elisha's gifts from God. Most likely her husband had told her of the mighty things he had seen the prophet do. Elisha was with the prophet Elijah when he struck the water of the Jordan River and the two crossed on dry ground. God also used Elisha to miraculously purify the water for a town plagued with bad water. This widow knew that God used Elisha in great ways. In her desperation she cried out to this man of God for help.

Elisha asked her a simple question: "How can I help you? Tell me, what do you have in your house?"[2] Notice Elisha was only concerned about what she had. He didn't want to know what she had lost or didn't have. He simply asked, "What do you have?" Isn't that the question we ought to be asking ourselves as well? Instead of being concerned with what we don't have or what other people have, we must focus on that simple question: What do we have?

Remember the little boy in the large crowd Jesus taught? Everyone was hungry, and the disciples suggested Jesus send everyone home so they could buy something for themselves. He replied by saying, "You give them something to eat."[3] Wait a minute. What did He mean? They didn't have anything to feed such a huge crowd.

But it was a great challenge because it made them stop and think, *Well, what* do *we have?* The disciples found a boy with two loaves and five fishes, yet wondered, "How far will this go among so many?" Oh, but they forgot who they were with. The God who can take little and make much. The God who is able to calm the sea and turn the water into wine and heal the sick. He is not concerned with what we don't have; He is concerned about what we do have that we are willing to offer to Him.

Sometimes we can become so consumed with what we have lost or will never get that we lose sight of what we have been given. That's one reason why I write out at least five things I'm thankful for each morning. It always turns out to be much more than five things, and when I'm through with my joy-filled list I always realize how very blessed I am. It's an opportunity to focus on what I do have and what I have been given. If you were asked the question Elisha asked the widow—"What do you have?"—would you be able to quickly rattle off a list because you have been continually thanking the Lord?

Adding Resources

Even in our challenges we can thank the Lord for what we do have. In my daily thankfulness list, I always try to thank Him for at least one challenge or disappointment in my life. If nothing more, it is an opportunity to trust Him through the difficulty. Often when I thank Him for something slightly imperfect in my life, I begin to see the benefit or the lesson learned or the growth that can take place. I don't know if Mrs. Prophet-widow was taking a daily inventory of what she did have, but when Elisha inquired what she had in her house she said, "Your servant has nothing there at all, except a little oil."

That's all Elisha needed to hear! She did have something, and the something was enough to multiply into something more. I love God's multiplication. Our little something, multiplied by His mighty power, can go much farther and wider than we ever imagined. Elisha told Mrs. Prophet-widow…wait, let's call her Penelope for now. That sounds so much better. Elisha told Penelope, "Go around and ask your neighbors for empty jars. Don't ask for just a few. Then go inside and shut the door behind you and your sons. Pour oil into all the jars, and as each is filled, put it to one side."[4]

Elisha knew she would need the help of others. He knew there were resources available to her, so he instructed her to seek them out. There is a message here for all of us "independent types" who think we can do it all ourselves. God provides resources beyond just our own gifts and talents, and we must reach out for those as well. The instructions were to reach out and connect with the resources of others. For some of us it is easy to just think we can do it better on our own. But no—God loves community and He wants us to connect. When we bring others into our projects and we serve others in theirs, the joy is spread all around.

Granted, there's always that flipside of being too dependent on or too needy of others. We don't want to constantly bother others with our troubles or ongoing needs. There is a healthy balance, and I believe that balance comes in as we seek the Lord first and follow His direction. He will lead us to the right resources, as well as the beautiful balance of using what we already have.

Now I want you to catch a bright glimmer of Penelope's faith. As Elisha told her to get as many jars as possible and begin pouring oil into them, you might think she would respond, "Are you kidding? Didn't you hear me? There's hardly any oil left. How could I pour it in these other jars?" Thankfully that wasn't Penelope's response. No, the Bible simply tells us she left him. I think she was ready to move forward in faith. I think she knew that God had something big in store. We don't know how many jars she gathered, but we do know she began pouring...and pouring and pouring.

Time Alone

An interesting little side note. Just this morning as I began writing this very chapter, I opened a devotional I love to read each day. It's one that has been around for many years, called *Streams in the Desert*, and it brings readings each day from a variety of sources and authors, all focusing on walking in faith especially in difficult times. Much to my amazement, the devotion for this morning was on the story of Elisha, the widow, and the oil. What's more, the author brought out a point I had not even considered.

It focused on Elisha's instruction to "go inside and shut the door behind you and your sons." Here's an excerpt:

> The widow and her two sons were to be alone with God. They were not dealing with the laws of nature, human government, the church, or the priesthood. Nor were they even dealing with God's great prophet Elisha. They had to be isolated from everyone, separated from human reasoning and removed from the natural tendencies to prejudge their circumstance. They were to be as if cast into the vast expanse of starry space, depending on God alone—in touch with the Source of miracles.
>
> This is an ingredient in God's plan of dealing with us. We are to enter a secret chamber of isolation in prayer and faith that is very fruitful. At certain times and places, God will build a mysterious wall around

us. He will take away all the supports we customarily lean upon, and will remove our ordinary ways of doing things. God will close us off to something divine, completely new and unexpected, and that cannot be understood by examining our previous circumstances. We will be in a place where we do not know what is happening, where God is cutting the cloth of our lives by a new pattern, and thus where He causes us to look to Him.

Most Christians lead a treadmill life—a life in which they can predict almost everything that will come their way. But the souls that God leads into unpredictable and special situations are isolated by Him. All they know is that God is holding them and that He is dealing in their lives. Then their expectations come from Him alone.

Like this widow, we must be detached from outward things and attached inwardly to the Lord alone in order to see His wonders.[5]

Honestly, I had never noticed this aspect of the story, yet what an important part to contemplate. We learned earlier of the importance of reaching out to others and connecting with one another, but it is even more vital that we spend time alone with God. As we commune with Him, our faith grows. As we learn from Him, we focus on what He is able to do. As we abide with Him, we become fruitful. Jesus said that He is the vine and we are the branches. He told us to remain, abide, dwell with Him—and as we do, we will bear much fruit. He added, "Apart from me you can do nothing."[6]

There is a danger of going and doing and connecting and yet never being still and alone with Him. We must be cautious of depending on others to feed us and help us grow spiritually. Yes, community is important, but alone time with the Father is essential. Make it a priority. Penelope went into her home and shut the door. She got rid of all the distractions because this was between her and God. His work, His way, alone with her faith and what little she had to offer. Each pot she gathered represented a portion of her faith. It was inside, alone with Him, that she began to pour, and He began to multiply.

My friend, do not neglect time alone with Him. Carve it into your schedule and make it an essential priority in your life. As I picture Penelope's little dwelling place, it offers beautiful imagery of Jesus' invitation to us: "Abide (dwell, remain) in me." In Revelation we read Jesus' words to the church at Laodicea: "Here I am! I stand at the door and knock. If anyone hears my voice and opens the door, I will come in and eat with that person, and they with me."[7] Oh, how wonderful to fellowship with our Lord! Oh, how sweet the time alone with Him can be. Oh, the great miracles that can happen as a result! Open the door of your heart and commune with Him.

Our Generous God

You've probably guessed the end of the story. Penelope began pouring and didn't stop until the last jar was full. After filling all the jars to the brim, I wonder if she said, "Crumb! We should have found more jars!" Or if she rejoiced because she had gathered all the jars she possibly could find and was overwhelmed with the results. We do know she went to tell Elisha about the wonderful bounty. He told her to go sell the oil and pay her debts and live on the rest. There was obviously more than enough oil for her needs! God poured out

His gifts to Penelope and her sons, lavishly and generously. The gifts were limited only by the number of jars she gathered.

I rejoice in the generosity of our God. He is not stingy. He is generous and gracious. He is generous with His love toward His own, He is generous with His grace, and He is generous with His wisdom. John, the beloved disciple, wrote, "See what great love the Father has lavished on us, that we should be called children of God! And that is what we are!"[8] The word *lavished* communicates "generous—no holding back." He does not hold back His love toward us as His children; He is generous with it.

Paul wrote to the church in Ephesus, "In him we have redemption through his blood, the forgiveness of sins, in accordance with the riches of God's grace that he lavished on us."[9] There's that word *lavish* again! He generously bestows His grace upon those who believe in Christ. We are forgiven by Christ's blood shed on the cross for us. God the Father isn't "sort of" gracious with us. He doesn't give us a little bit of grace here and there. No, He is overflowing with grace! He is rich with grace, and He pours out His gracious mercy and kindness in abundant supply.

Finally, God generously gives us wisdom when we ask Him for it. He is a giving God and wants to bestow direction and guidance upon us when we seek His help. James wrote, "If any of you lacks wisdom, you should ask God, who gives generously to all without finding fault, and it will be given to you."[10]

I find myself strengthened and encouraged by the fact that from His glorious riches God lavishes His love, His grace, and His wisdom upon us. There is no limit to His power, and there is no limit to what He can do through His beloved children.

What about you? Do you believe God can use you to make a difference in people's lives? Do you believe He can use your gifts and talents, despite your inabilities or weaknesses, despite your past? Do you believe He created you for a purpose and will work beyond your limitations to fulfill that purpose? Are you willing to invite Him to do mighty things in you and through you? Believe big! Believe that He can use you in wonderful and meaningful ways. Believe that He hears your prayers and will provide what is best for you. Believe that He is good and has a good plan. Our Father, who dearly loves us, has unlimited resources. Seek His help in every area of your life.

Positive Life Strategy

POWERFUL TRUTH

Believe that when we give God what little we have,
He can do great and mighty things.

PLAN OF ACTION

1. Go to God with your needs.

2. Take a daily inventory of what you do have by counting your blessings each morning.

3. Make use of the resources God places around you.

4. Spend time alone with Him, seeking His help and guidance.

5. Step forward in faith. Don't limit the possibilities.

Pay It Forward

Do you know someone who is struggling with believing God and trusting Him through difficulties? Help them believe big by reminding them of the stories and scriptures from this chapter as well as praying with them. Ask the Lord to give them strength and peace, but more importantly ask Him for wisdom as they take steps forward each day. Remind them they never know what is around the corner, and remind them to, as Billy Ray put it, "let God do the work." Help them to trust that His plan is a good plan, and He can do more than we ask or imagine.

Place It in Your Heart

By his divine power, God has given us everything we need for living a godly life. We have received all of this by coming to know him.

2 Peter 1:3-4 NLT

Discussion Starters

- Tell about a time in your life when God did much more than you asked or imagined.

- What keeps us from believing big at times?

Eight Transforming Truths
That Can Change Your Life

It is not my ability,
but my response to God's ability,
that counts.

CORRIE TEN BOOM

Here's your final charge—your motivational recap—your positive push to move you forward! Using the principles we learned in this book, I want to give you an at-a-glance reminder to help you as you continue on your journey. Remember you are not alone—your loving heavenly Father walks with you each step of the way.

1. Keep your thinking right. Only dwell on what is true, noble, and right.

2. Keep your focus on the possibilities. Don't get distracted by your difficulties.

3. Keep running your race. Don't be discouraged by comparing yourself with others.

4. Keep your criticism in check. Give more encouragement than discouragement.

5. Keep a courageous spirit. Fight against worry and fears with faith.

6. Keep reaching out to others. Step out of your comfort zone to be a blessing.

7. Keep a proactive attitude. Guard against knee-jerk reactions. Respond wisely.

8. Keep believing big. Trust a great God to do great things.

For more positive encouragement from Karol,
go to her website at www.PositiveLifePrinciples.com.

Additional Resources

There are a plethora of positive stories of success, far more than could fit in the pages of this book. I want to encourage you to explore the following books and enjoy learning from other women who have found strength and victory despite the challenges they have faced in life. Here are some of my favorites:

- *A Chance to Die: The Life and Legacy of Amy Carmichael,* Elisabeth Elliot, Revell Publishers, 2005.

- *Self Talk, Soul Talk: What to Say When You Talk to Yourself,* Jennifer Rothschild, Harvest House, 2007.

- *Thrive, Don't Simply Survive: Passionately Live the Life You Didn't Plan,* Karol Ladd, Howard Books, 2009.

- *Trusting God in Times of Adversity: [The Book of] Job,* Kay Arthur, Harvest House, 2003.

- *A Lineage of Grace: Five Stories of Unlikely Women who Changed Eternity,* Francine Rivers, Tyndale, 2009.

Notes

Chapter 1—Listen to the Right Voices

1. A.W. Tozer, as quoted in *The Westminster Collection of Christian Quotations,* Martin H. Manser, comp. (Louisville, KY: Westminster John Knox Press, 2001), p. 376.

2. Genesis 3:1-7.

3. 1 Peter 5:8 NLT.

4. Philippians 2:13.

5. Psalm 23 NLT.

6. John 15:9.

7. 1 John 3:1 NLT.

Chapter 2—Look for the Possibilities

1. 2 Samuel 23:20.

2. Psalm 103:4.

3. Lamentations 3:19-20 NLT.

4. Lamentations 3:21-25 NLT.

5. Psalm 34:5.

6. Genesis 18:9-15 NLT.

Chapter 3—Guard Against Comparisons

1. Philippians 3:14.

2. Genesis 29:32-35.

3. Genesis 30:1-2.

4. *More Gathered Gold,* John Blanchard, ed. (Hertfordshire, England: Evangelical Press, 1986), p. 84.

5. Romans 12:15 ESV.

Chapter 4—Be an Encourager, Not a Discourager

1. Numbers 12:1-3 NLT.

2. Numbers 12:4-10 NLT.

3. Numbers 12:10-13 NLT.

4. Luke 6:27-28.

5. Proverbs 15:4.

6. James 3:7-8.

7. Psalm 19:14 NLT.

Chapter 5—Face Your Fears

1. Esther 4:11.

2. Esther 4:13-14.

3. Esther 4:16.

4. James 1:2-8.

5. Psalm 23:4 NLT.

6. Joshua 1:8-9.

7. Proverbs 9:10.

8. 2 Chronicles 20:2-4.

9. 2 Chronicles 20:5-12.

10. 2 Chronicles 20:13-17.

11. 2 Chronicles 20:18-19.

12. 2 Chronicles 20:20-23.

Chapter 6—Reach Out and Help Others

1. I sponsor a child and missionary through Gospel for Asia (www.GFA.org) and also World Vision (www.worldvision.org).

2. Ruth 1:16-18.

3. Ruth 2:11-12.

4. Psalm 36:5-9.

5. See Leviticus 25:25.

6. Philippians 2:5-8.

7. John 15:13.

8. Proverbs 31:20,25,29.

9. Proverbs 31:30-31.

Chapter 7—Be Proactive Rather Than Reactive

1. 1 Samuel 25:10-11.

2. 1 Samuel 25:14-17.

3. 1 Samuel 25:32-35.

4. 1 Samuel 25:28-31.

5. A.M. Overton, "He Maketh No Mistake," 1932. See www.churchlead.com/mind_wanderings/view/1630/ for the story behind this poem, as told by the author's grandson, Rob Overton.

Chapter 8—Believe Big

1. *More Gathered Gold,* John Blanchard, ed. (Hertfordshire, England: Evangelical Press, 1986), p. 116.

2. 2 Kings 4:2.

3. Mark 6:37.

4. 2 Kings 4:3-4.

5. *Streams in the Desert,* L.B. Cowman, comp. (Grand Rapids, MI: Zondervan Publishers, 1997), p. 143.

6. John 15:5.

7. Revelation 3:20.

8. 1 John 3:1.

9. Ephesians 1:7-8.

10. James 1:5.

About the Author

Karol Ladd is known as the "Positive Lady." Her unique gift of encouraging women from the truths of God's Word, as well as her enthusiasm and joy, is evident in both her speaking and her writing.

Karol is the bestselling author of over 25 books, including *The Power of a Positive Mom*, *A Woman's Passionate Pursuit of God* (book and DVD), *A Woman's Secret to Confident Living* (book and DVD), and *Unfailing Love*. She is a gifted Bible teacher and popular speaker to women's organizations, church groups, and corporate events across the nation. Karol is also a frequent guest on radio and television, sharing a message of joy and strength found in the Lord. Her most valued role is that of wife to Curt and mother to daughters Grace and Joy.

Visit her website at **www.PositiveLifePrinciples.com** for daily doses of encouragement and more information on how you can start your own Positive Woman Connection Bible Study.

Also by Karol Ladd

A Woman's Passionate Pursuit of God
(book and DVD)
Creating a Positive and Purposeful Life

As you explore Paul's intriguing letter to the Philippians with popular author and speaker Karol Ladd, you'll learn to live intentionally as you face life's daily challenges. Most important, you'll be helped to understand God's Word and His plans for your life and say more and more, "Father, I want what You want."

Filled with inspiring true-life stories, practical steps, and study questions, this book is perfect for personal quiet times, a book club pick, or a group Bible study.

It's complemented by the DVD version, offering six 30-minute sessions from Karol, a helpful leader's guide, and discussion questions. *Excellent for small-group or church class study.*

A Woman's Secret for Confident Living
(book and DVD)
Becoming Who God Made You to Be

Bestselling author Karol Ladd shares powerful truths from the book of Colossians to help you make a vital shift in perspective. Knowing Christ and His greatness, and knowing who you are in Him, sets you on an exciting path to living—not in self-confidence, but *God*-confidence. You'll be helped to do the following:

- get rid of negative and self-defeating thoughts

- cultivate your potential, because you're valuable to Him

- shine with joy and assurance of what you bring to the world

Includes questions to bring depth and dimension to individual or group study.

In the complementary DVD version, Karol digs transforming truth out of the Scriptures in six positive, inspiring sessions such as "Transform Your Thinking," "Grow in Christ," and "Strengthen Your Relationships." *Helpful leader's guide included for group use.*

Unfailing Love
A Woman's Walk Through First John

It's easy to talk about filling your heart with God's love, but it's another thing to embrace His love, feel it, and allow it to color the fabric of your life. In this insightful journey through 1 John, Karol Ladd invites you to experience the reality of God's generous love. As you begin to grasp its height and depth...

- you're transformed, seeing yourself and your circumstances in a fresh new light.

- you get a truer picture of Jesus, God's Son, in a way that helps you navigate the false loves, temporary pleasures, and seductions of today's culture.

- you're able to graciously, compassionately, and creatively love others by your words and actions.

God is Light, Life, and Love. As you embrace Him, you'll experience how He gives meaning to your existence, victory over your discouragements, and hope to the world.

Pursuing God in the Quiet Places

Every aspect of God's nature and character is an encouragement and a reason to be grateful. The more you know about Him, the more you will experience His joy.

Revel in His presence, character, and love in this fresh gathering of intimate devotions. Each meditation illumines a character quality of God from the Scriptures, igniting praise and admiration for the One who cares so much about you.

As you come to know and understand Him better, your heart and life will overflow with love—His love—throughout your day.

To learn more about Harvest House books and
to read sample chapters, log on to our website:

www.harvesthousepublishers.com

HARVEST HOUSE PUBLISHERS
EUGENE, OREGON